2·50

CHOOSING A NAME
FOR YOUR BABY

D0928567

CHOOSING A NAME FOR YOUR BABY

PENGUIN BOOKS

PENGUIN BOOKS

Published by the Penguin Group
Penguin Books Ltd, 27 Wrights Lane, London W8 5TZ, England
Penguin Books USA Inc., 375 Hudson Street, New York, New York 10014, USA
Penguin Books Australia Ltd, Ringwood, Victoria, Australia
Penguin Books Canada Ltd, 10 Alcorn Avenue, Toronto, Ontario, Canada M4V 3B2
Penguin Books (NZ) Ltd, 182–190 Wairau Road, Auckland 10, New Zealand

Penguin Books Ltd, Registered Offices: Harmondsworth, Middlesex, England

First published by Penguin Books 1992
Reprinted with minor revisions 1994
1 3 5 7 9 10 8 6 4 2

Copyright © Penguin Books Australia Ltd, 1992
All rights reserved

Filmset in 10/12 ITC Cheltenham by
Rowlands Phototypesetting Ltd, Bury St Edmunds, Suffolk

Printed in England by Clays Ltd, St Ives plc

Except in the United States of America, this book is sold subject
to the condition that it shall not, by way of trade or otherwise, be lent,
re-sold, hired out, or otherwise circulated without the publisher's
prior consent in any form of binding or cover other than that in
which it is published and without a similar condition including this
condition being imposed on the subsequent purchaser

CONTENTS

Introduction   vii

Girls' Names   **1**

Boys' Names   **63**

INTRODUCTION

Names are important. They give a person an identity, an image and a sense of confidence. So make sure you take the time, in the months before the birth, to enjoy the pleasure of finding the right name for your very special baby.

Remember that the name you choose for your child should harmonise with your surname. Often a short given name goes well with a long surname and vice versa. A given name with an ending similar to the beginning of the surname – for example, Joshua Alexander – can sound awkward, as can names, such as Sally O'Malley, that are too alike.

Remember, too, that at school children are often given nicknames and abbreviations based on their names: you may love Alice but hate the shortened version Al. Richard Head may live to regret his parents' vagueness or naivety, and Donald Owen Grant and his sister Penelope Iris may find their initials the butt of many jokes!

A name that is the height of fashion today can quickly be outdated or inappropriate tomorrow. An unusual name can be charming to possess; an eccentric one will be a burden to bear. Remember, above all, that a name lasts a lifetime – and that a name wisely chosen is one of the most precious gifts you can give your child.

GIRLS' NAMES

A

Abbey *see* Abigail

Abella (Latin) beautiful

Abigail (Hebrew) a father's joy
Also Abaigael, Abbey, Abby,
Abigal, Gail
See also Gail

Abra (Hebrew) mother of
multitudes

Acacia (Greek) flower name

Ada (Old German) prosperous
and happy
Also Adda, Aida, Eda, Etta

Adah (Hebrew) ornament

Adamina (Scottish) from the
Hebrew for 'of the red earth'
Feminine form of Adam

Adela (Old German) *see* Adèle

Adelaide (Old German) of
noble rank
Also Adalia, Adaline, Adelaida,
Adelheid, Adelia, Adelina,
Adeline, Alina, Aline, Alyna
See also Adèle, Alice

Adèle (French) from the Old
German for 'of noble cheer'
Also Adela, Adelie, Adella,
Adelle, Adila, Edila, Edla
See also Adelaide, Alice

Adeline *see* Adelaide

Adonia (Greek) beautiful,
goddess-like lady
Feminine form of Adonis

Adriana (Latin) woman of the
Adriatic
Feminine form of Adrian
Also Adria, Adriane, Adrianna,
Adrianne, Adrienne

Adrienne (French) *see* Adriana

Affrica (Celtic) pleasant

Agatha (Greek) good, kind
woman
Also Agace, Agacia, Agafia,
Agata, Agathe, Agathy, Ageuda

Aglaia (Greek) splendour,
beauty; one of the three
Graces – goddess of harmony
Also Aglae

Agnes (Greek) pure, chaste
Also Agna, Agnella, Agnese,
Agneta, Agnete, Agnies,
Agnyta, Aigneis, Aneda, Anese,
Annais, Anneyce, Annis,
Annys, Ines, Inesita, Inez,
Nesta, Neysa, Neza, Ynes,
Ynez

Agnies (French) *see* Agnes

Agnola (Italian) *see* Angela

Agostina (Italian) *see* Augusta

Ah Cy (Chinese) lovely
Ah Lam (Chinese) like the orchid
Aileen (Anglo–Irish) *see* Helen
Ailsa (Scottish) of good cheer
 Also Aillsa, Ailssa, Elsa, Ilsa
Aimée (French) *see* Amy
Ainsley (Old English) clearing
 or meadow
 Also Ainslea, Ainslee,
 Ainsleigh, Ainsly, Anslea
Airlia (Greek) ethereal
Aithne (Celtic) little fire
 Also Eithne, Ethene, Ethne
Alana (Celtic) beautiful,
 harmonious one
 Feminine form of Alan
 Also Alaine, Alanah, Alanna,
 Alanne, Alayna, Alayne,
 Aleine, Alina, Aline, Allene,
 Allyn, Lana, Lane, Lanna
Alatea (Spanish) truth
Alberta (Old German) noble
 and bright
 Feminine form of Albert
 Also Albertina, Albertine,
 Albertyna, Albrette, Elberta
Albinia (Latin) *see* Elvira
 Also Alba, Albigna, Albina
Alcestis (Greek) A loyal wife, or
 a heroic woman
Alda (Old German) old
Alethea (Greek) truth
 Also Alatea, Aleethea, Aletea,
 Aletha, Aletheia, Alithea

Aletta (Latin) winged or bird-
 like
 Also Aleta, Alette, Alida, Alita,
 Alouetta
Alexandra (Greek) helper and
 protector of mankind
 Feminine form of Alexander
 Also Alejandra, Aleksandrina,
 Alessandra, Alexa,
 Alexandraine, Alexandria,
 Alexandrina, Alexandrine,
 Alexia, Alexina, Alexine,
 Alexis, Alix, Elexa, Sacha,
 Sandra, Sondra, Zandra
Alexia *see* Alexandra
Alexis *see* Alexandra
Alfreda (Old German) elf
 counsel
 Feminine form of Alfred
 Also Albreda, Alfreta
Alice (Old German) noble and
 kind
 Also Ailis, Aleece, Alesia,
 Alicen, Alicia, Alis, Alisa, Alise,
 Alison, Alisone, Alisoun,
 Alisson, Alize, Allis, Allisa,
 Allissa, Allysa, Allyson, Alson,
 Alyce, Alys, Lycia
 See also Adelaide, Adèle
Alicia *see* Alice
Alina (Latin) *see* Adelaide
 (Adeline)
 See also Alana
Alison (Gaelic) *see* Alice

Alivia (Old English) alive

Alix (French) *see* Alexandra

Alla (Old English) the only one

Allegra (Italian) joyful and cheerful

Allonia (Hebrew) oak tree
Feminine form of Alon
Also Alona

Alma (Latin) fair or kind
Also Elma

Almeria (Old German) hard-working ruler
Feminine form of Almeric

Almira (Arabic) princess
Also Almeria, Elmira, Mira

Alouetta *see* Aletta

Alpha (Greek) the first

Althea (Greek) wholesome, a healer
Also Althaea, Althee, Altheta, Thea

Alvira *see* Elvira

Alwyn (Old German) elf friend

Alysia (Greek) possessive
Also Alisa, Alisia, Alysa

Alyssa (Greek) flower name, Alyssum

Alzena (Arabic) woman

Amabel *see* Mabel

Amanda (Latin) worthy of love

Amara (Greek) unfolding

Amara (Sanskrit) immortal

Amaranth (Greek) fading flower
Also Amarantha

Amarinda (Greek) long-lived, beauty which does not fade
Also Armargo

Amaryllis (Greek) country girl; sparkling stream
Also Amarilla, Amarillis, Amaryl, Marilla

Amata (Latin) *see* Amy

Amber (Egyptian) light

Amelia (Old German) *see* Emily

Amena (Old French) yielding

Amethyst (Greek) of the colour of wine

Aminar (Arabic) honest, faithful

Aminta (Greek) protected

Amity (French) friendly

Amy (French) beloved
Also Aimée, Amata, Amaya, Ame, Amia, Amice, Amie, Amieia, Amina, Amity, Amoretta, Amorita, Amye, Esmé, Esmée

Anais (English) *see* Anne

Anastasia (Greek) resurrection
Feminine form of Anastasius
Also Anastasie, Anastassia, Anastatia, Anastazia, Anestasia, Anstace, Anstey, Anstice, Anstyce, Nastassia, Nastassja, Nastassla, Nastasya, Nastaya, Nastya, Nastyenka, Stacia, Stacie, Stacy, Tasia

Andrea (Greek) womanly
Feminine form of Andrew
(Andreas)
Also Aindrea, Andreana,
Andrée, Andria, Andriana,
Andrina

Angela (Greek) a heavenly
messenger
Feminine form of Angel
Also Agnola, Aingeal, Angel,
Angele, Angeletta, Angelina,
Angeline, Angelita, Angiola,
Aniela, Anjela, Engel,
Engelchen

Angelica (Latin) angelic
Also Angelika, Angelique,
Angyelika

Angelina (English) *see* Angela

Anita *see* Anne

Annabel (Scottish) *see* Mabel
(Amabel)

Anne (Hebrew) full of grace
Also Ana, Anais, Anca, Aneta,
Anica, Anita, Ann, Anna,
Annan, Annetta, Annette,
Annie, Annika, Annina,
Annuschka, Anona, Chana,
Channa, Hana, Hanicka,
Hanita, Hannah, Hannette,
Nan, Nancy, Nanette, Nanny,
Nina, Ninette, Nita, Ona,
Vanka

Annette (French) *see* Anne

Annora *see* Honora

Anthea (Greek) lady of the
flowers
Also Anthia, Bluma, Thea, Thia

Antigone (Greek) contrary,
born against

Antoinette (French) *see* Antonia

Antonia (Italian) from the Latin
for 'inestimable, beyond price'
Feminine form of Anthony
(Antony)
Also Anthonia, Antoinette,
Antonette, Antoni, Antonya,
Netta, Netti, Netty, Toinette,
Toni, Tonya

Aphra (Hebrew) dust
Also Afra

Appolline (Greek) of Apollo
Also Apollonia

April (Latin) the open
Also Avril

Arabella (Latin) beautiful altar;
moved by prayer
Also Belle, Bella, Oriabel

Araminta *combination* of
Arabella and Aminta

Arcadia (Greek) peaceful and
happy

Areta (Greek) holy, virtuous,
divine
Also Arete, Aretha, Aretta,
Arette

Ariadne (Greek) the very holy
one
Also Ariadna, Ariane, Arianna

Ariel (Hebrew) lioness of God
Also Ariella, Arielle

Arleen (Old German) a pledge

Armida (Persian) beautiful
sorceress

Armilda (Latin) braceleted

Arrabel (Scottish) *see* Mabel
(Amabel)

Asha (African) life
Also Aisha

Ashleigh (Old English) of the
ash tree
Also Ashlee

Aspasia (Greek) welcome

Asta (Greek) a star

Astrid (Old German) divine
strength

Asura (Sanskrit) spiritual

Atalanta (Greek) swift runner
Also Atalante, Atalanti,
Attalanta

Atalaya (Spanish) watcher,
guardian
Also Ataliah, Atalya, Talia,
Talya

Athanasia (Greek) undying,
immortal

Athena (Greek) wisdom
Also Athene

Audrey (Old English) noble
strength
Also Audrea, Audree, Audrie,
Audrye, Etheldreda

Augusta (Latin) the high,
honoured, mighty
Feminine form of Augustus
Also Agostina, Augusteen,
Augustina, Augustine, Austina,
Austine, Gus, Gussie, Gusta,
Tina

Aurelia (Latin) golden lady
Also Aralie, Aurea, Aurel,
Aurelie

Aurora (Latin) dawn
Also Aurore, Ora

Ava (Greek) eagle

Avalon (Latin) island
Also Avallon

Aveline (Hebrew) pleasant

Averil (Old English) sacred wild
boar

Avicia (German) *see* Avis

Avis (Old German) bird-
like
Also Aricia, Avice,
Avicia

Ayesha (Persian) happy

Azalea (Old German) of noble
cheer
Also Azaleah

Azaria (Hebrew) blessed by
God
Feminine form of Azariah
Also Azeria, Zaria

Aziza (African) gorgeous

Azura (Persian) sky blue

B

Babette (French) *see* Barbara

Baptista (Old French) one who baptises
Feminine form of Baptist
Also Baptysta, Batista, Battista

Barbara (Greek) stranger
Also Babette, Babica, Barbe, Barbrischa, Barbro, Baruska, Varenka, Varina, Varvara

Basia *see* Basilia

Basilia (Greek) royal
Feminine form of Basil
Also Basia, Basilea, Basilie, Basilla

Bassania (Greek) realm of the sea

Bathsheba (Hebrew) daughter of a vow
Also Sheba

Beatrice (Latin) she who brings joy
Also Beatrix, Beatriz, Beatty, Blaza, Blazena, Trixie

Bebe (French) baby

Beka (Hebrew) half-sister
Also Becca, Bekah, Bekka

Belinda (Old German) wise serpent
Also Belynda
See also Linda, Melinda

Belisama (Gaelic) queen of heaven

Belle (French) beautiful
Also Bell, Bella
See also Arabella, Elizabeth (Isabel), Mabel (Annabel, Arrabel), Mirabel

Belvina (Latin) fair one
Also Belva, Belvia

Benedicta (Latin) the blessed
Feminine form of Benedict
Also Benedetta, Benedikta, Benetta, Benicia, Benita, Benoîte

Benita (Spanish) *see* Benedicta

Berengaria (Old German) a bear, spear
Feminine form of Berenger

Berenice (Greek) bringer of victory
Also Berneice, Bernice, Berniz, Berrice

Bernadette (Old German) as brave as a bear
Feminine form of Bernard
Also Bernadina, Bernadine, Bernadot, Bernadotte, Bernetta, Bernita, Burnette

Bertha (Old German) the bright
 Also Berta, Berthe, Bertilia,
 Bertina, Bertine
Beryl (Greek) precious jewel,
 precious stone
 Also Beryle, Berylla
Bessie *see* Elizabeth
Beth *see* Elizabeth
Bethany (Hebrew) worshipper
 of God
 Also Bethanie
Bethia (Hebrew) daughter of
 Jehovah
Bettina *see* Elizabeth
Beulah (Hebrew) to be married
 Also Beula, Beulie
Beverley (Old English) from the
 beaver's stream
 Also Beverlie
Bianca (Italian) *see* Blanche
Bibiana (Latin) full of life
 Also Bibi, Viviana
Bijou (French) jewel
Birget (German) *see* Bridget
Birgitta (Scandinavian) *see*
 Bridget
Blanche (French) white
 Also Bianca, Bijanka, Blanca,
 Blanch, Blanka, Bluinse,
 Branca
Blasia (Latin) the babbler
Bliss (Old English) felicity,
 happiness
Blodwen (Welsh) white flower

Blossom (Old English) plant or
 tree in flower
Blythe (Old English) happy and
 joyous
Bo (Chinese) precious
Bobbette *see* Roberta
Bonnie (Latin) good
 Also Bona, Bonita, Bonny
Branwen (Welsh) dark-haired
 beauty
Breanna *see* Bryony
Brenda (Old English) firebrand
 or sword
Brenna (Celtic) dark-haired
Briana (Celtic) woman of
 strength
 Feminine form of Brian
 Also Brianna, Brienne
Bridget (Celtic) the highest
 strength
 Also Bedelia, Beret, Birget,
 Birgitta, Bride, Bridgid, Bridie,
 Brie, Bries, Brietta, Briganti,
 Brigette, Brighid, Brigid,
 Brigida, Brigide, Brigit, Brigita,
 Brigitta, Brigitte, Brigyta,
 Brischia, Brit, Brita, Britt,
 Britta
Brie *see* Bridget
Briony *see* Bryony
Britt *see* Bridget
Bronwen (Celtic) the white
 breast
 Also Bronwyn

Brooke (Old English) at the brook

Bryony (Old English) to swell or grow; a plant name
Also Breanna, Brianne, Briony

C

Caitlin (Irish) *see* Catherine

Calandra (Greek) a lark

Callista (Greek) most beautiful

Callula (Latin) beautiful little girl

Calpurnia (Latin) the name of Julius Caesar's wife
Also Calphurnia

Calypso (Greek) to cover, conceal

Camilla (Etruscan) attendant at religious ceremonies
Also Camellia, Camila, Camille, Kamila, Kamilla

Candace (Greek) glittering white or glowing
Also Candice, Candida, Candide

Cara (Italian) dearest one
Also Carina, Carita, Kara
See also Caroline

Carissa (Latin) artful or skilful
Also Carisa, Chrissa

Carla (English) *see* Caroline

Carlotta *see* Charlotte

Carly (German) free woman
Also Carla, Carley, Carlita, Karla

Carma (Sanskrit) destiny

Carmel (Hebrew) vineyard or garden
Also Carmela, Carmelina, Carmeline, Carmelita, Melina

Carmen (Spanish) songstress
Also Carmena, Carmencita, Carmia, Carmina, Carmine, Carmita, Charmain, Charmaine

Carol (Old French) to sing joyously
Also Carola, Carole, Caroll, Karel, Karol
See also Caroline

Caroline (Latin) virile and strong
Feminine form of Charles (Carolus)
Also Caddie, Cara, Carla, Carlina, Carline, Carlita, Carolina, Carolyn, Charleen, Charlene, Karla, Karolina, Karoline, Karoly, Karolyn, Sharleen, Sharlene
See also Carol

Casey (Irish) courageous, brave

Casilda (Spanish) solitary one
Also Casilde, Cassilda

Casimira (Polish) bearer of peace
Feminine form of Casimir

Cassandra (Greek) confuser of men; one who excites love
Also Casandra, Cassandre, Kassandra

Catarina (Italian) *see* Catherine

Catherine (Greek) pure
Also Caireen, Cairine, Caitlin, Caitlyn, Caitrin, Caren, Carin, Cartlin, Catalina, Catarzyna, Cateline, Caterina, Caterine, Catharine, Cathelina, Catherina, Catheryn, Cathleen, Cathren, Catlin, Catriona, Cattarina, Kaarina, Kaatje, Kadi, Kajsa, Kalina, Kara, Karen, Karena, Karia, Karina, Karlinka, Karyna, Kasche, Kasia, Kasse, Kassia, Kata, Katalin, Katarzyna, Katchen, Kate, Katerina, Katerine, Kateryn, Katharine, Katherine, Kathleen, Kathryn, Kathy, Katie, Katina, Katinka, Katka, Katren, Katri, Katrina, Katrine, Katti, Katura, Katushka, Katy, Katya, Kitty
See also Kay

Cecilia (Latin) blind
Feminine form of Cecil
Also Cacilia, Cecile, Cecilie, Cecilija, Cecily, Celia, Célie,
Cicely, Cilka, Sheelagh, Sheila, Sheilah, Shelagh, Sileas, Sycily

Celeste (Latin) heavenly
Also Celesta, Celestina, Celestine

Celia *see* Cecilia

Celina *see* Selena

Chanda (Sanskrit) destroyer of evil

Channa (Yiddish) *see* Anne

Chantal (French) singer
Also Chantalle, Chantel, Chantelle, Shantelle

Charis *see* Charity

Charity (Greek) love and grace
Also Charis, Charissa, Charita, Cherry

Charlotte (French) from the Latin for 'virile and strong'
Feminine form of Charles
Also Carla, Carleen, Carlina, Carlita, Carlotta, Charleen, Charlene, Charlotta, Karla, Karlotta, Lola

Charmaine (Greek) *see* Carmen

Charmian (Greek) a little joy
Also Charmion

Chen (Chinese) precious and rare

Chérie *see* Cheryl
Also Cher, Cheri

Cherry *see* Charity

Cheryl (French) dear, beloved
one
Also Cher, Cheri, Chérie,
Sharyl, Sherrill, Sherry,
Sheryl
Chiang (Chinese) name of last
queen of Yin dynasty
Chiquita (Spanish) little
Chispa (Spanish) a spark
Chloe (Greek) a young green
shoot
Chloris (Greek) pale flower,
fresh and blooming
Also Chloras, Clorita, Loris
Cho (Japanese) butterfly
Christabel (Greek) beautiful,
bright-faced Christian
Also Christabella, Christobel,
Cristabel
Christiana (Latin) *see* Christine
Christine (Greek) a Christian
Feminine form of Christian
Also Cairistine, Cairistiona,
Chris, Chrissie, Chrissy,
Christa, Christiana, Christiane,
Christie, Christina, Christinha,
Christie, Christina, Christinha,
Christophine, Christy, Cristin,
Cristina, Cristiona, Gristin,
Kirsten, Krista, Kristiana,
Kristin, Kristina
Chrystal *see* Crystal
Chu (Chinese) pearl
Chun (Chinese) spring

Cilla *see* Priscilla
Cindy *see* Lucy (Lucinda)
Claire *see* Clare
Clarabelle (Latin) the clear,
bright and beautiful
Also Clarabella, Claribel
Clare (Latin) clear and bright
Also Chiara, Chlaris, Claire,
Clairette, Clara, Claresta,
Clareta, Clarice, Clarinda,
Clarine, Clariss, Clarissa,
Clarisse, Clarita, Clarona,
Kara, Klara, Klarika, Klarissa
Clarice (French) *see* Clare
Clarimond (Old French) bright
protector
Also Clairmond
Clarinda (Spanish) *see* Clare
Clarissa *see* Clare
Claudia (Latin) the lame
Feminine form of Claude
(Claudius)
Also Claude, Claudette,
Claudina, Claudine, Clause,
Klaudia
Cleine (Greek) renowned
Clematis (Greek) flower name
meaning 'the clinging'
Clementine (Latin) the clement
or merciful
Feminine form of Clement
Also Clémence, Clemency,
Clementa, Clemente,
Clementia, Clementina,

Clemenza, Cleti, Klementina, Klementyna

Cleopatra (Greek) glory or fame
Also Cleo

Clodagh (Irish) name of a river in Tipperary

Clorinda (Persian) renowned

Clothilda (Old German) chief or leader's daughter
Also Clothilde, Clotilda, Klothilde

Clover (English) flower name
Also Claver

Colette *see* Nicole

Colleen (Irish) girl
Also Coleen, Colene

Columbine (Latin) dove; a flower name
Feminine form of Columba
Also Colombe, Columba, Columbia, Columbina

Conception (Latin) beginning
Also Concetta

Concetta (Italian) *see* Conception

Concha (Latin) shell
Also Conchita

Connor (Irish) high desire
Also Conor

Constance (Latin) firm in faith
Feminine form of Constantine
Also Concettina, Constancia, Constanta, Constantia, Constantina, Constanz, Constanza, Constanzia, Custance, Konstanca, Konstancia, Kostancia, Kostka

Consuelo (Latin) consolation
Also Consuela

Cora (Greek) young maiden
Also Corella, Corenna, Corenne, Coretta, Corette, Corianna, Corinna, Corinne, Corrie, Corry, Kora

Coral (Latin) charm
Also Coralie, Coralina, Coraline

Cordelia (Latin) sea jewel
Also Cordelie, Delia

Corinna *see* Cora

Cornelia (Latin) a horn
Feminine form of Cornelius

Cosette (Old German) pet lamb
Also Cosetta

Cosima (Greek) order and harmony

Cottina (Greek) crown of wild flowers

Courtney (Old French) dweller at court

Cressa (Old German) watercress

Cressida (Greek) uncertain origin; made famous in Shakespeare's *Troilus and Cressida*

Crystal (Greek) ice-clear
  Also Christel, Chrystal,
  Krystal
Custance (Old English) *see*
  Constance
Cynthia (Greek) the moon
  Also Cinta, Cynta, Cynthie

Cyrilla (Latin) high born, lordly
  lady
  Feminine form of Cyril
  Also Cyrille
Cythera (Greek) from Cythera
  Also Cytheria
Czenzi (Hungarian) increasing

D

Dacia (Greek) an ancient country north of the Danube
Also Dachia

Dagmar (Danish) glory of the Danes
Also Dagmara

Dahlia (Latin) flower name, of the valley

Daisy (Old English) day's eye, flower name

Dai-Tai (Chinese) spring

Dale (Old English) valley
Also Dayle

Dalila (African) gentle

Dallas (Old Irish) the skilled and wise

Damaris (Greek) tame or gentle
Also Damara

Damaspia (Persian) horse tamer

Damayanti (Sanskrit) pearl of girls

Dana *see* Danica

Danella *see* Daniela

Danette (Old German) little mistress
Also Danete, Danetta

Danica (Old Slavonic) the morning star

Also Dahna, Dana, Danah, Dayna

Daniela (Hebrew) God is my judge
Feminine form of Daniel
Also Danella, Danete, Danetta, Danette, Daniell, Danielle, Danila, Danita, Danka, Dannetej, Danya, Danye

Danielle (French) *see* Daniela

Daphne (Greek) bay or laurel, a flower name
Also Daphna

Dara (Hebrew) charity, compassion and wisdom
Also Darra

Darcie (Celtic) dark

Daria (Persian) queenly
Also Darice, Darya

Darlene (Old English) little darling
Also Darelle, Darleen

Davida *see* Davina

Davina (Scottish) from the Hebrew for 'beloved, loved by God'
Feminine form of David
Also Dainia, Davida, Davita, Vida, Vidette, Vita

Dawn (Old English) break of day
See also Aurora

Dea (Latin) goddess

Dealva (Latin) white

Deanna *see* Diana

Deborah (Hebrew) the bee, implying wisdom and eloquence
Also Deberah, Debora, Debra, Devora

Decima (Latin) the tenth child

Deirdre (Old Irish) sorrowing or broken-hearted

Delia (Greek) moon goddess
Also Delena
See also Cordelia

Delilah (Hebrew) the gentle temptress, desire
Also Lila

Della (Old German) noble

Delora (Latin) from the seashore
Also Ellora

Delores *see* Dolores

Delvine (Greek) of Delphi
Also Delfina, Delfine, Delphine

Denise (French) after the god of wine, Dionysos
Feminine form of Dennis (Dionysos)
Also Denice, Denys, Dione, Dionetta, Dionette, Dionis, Dionne, Dionycia, Dionysia

Desdemona (Greek) misery

Désirée (French) desired one
Also Desiderata, Desiderius

Desmia (Latin) a beautiful butterfly

Desolin (Old French) left alone

Deva (Sanskrit) divine shining light
Also Devi

Devona (Old English) of Devon

Diana (Latin) name of the goddess of the moon
Also Deana, Deane, Deanna, Deanne, Diahann, Diane, Dianna, Dyan, Dyana, Dyane, Dyann

Dido (Greek) teacher

Diella (Latin) worshipper of God

Dilys (Welsh) genuine, perfect
Also Delys

Dinah (Hebrew) the judged, vindicated
Also Dina, Dyna

Dione (Greek) *see* Denise

Dionysia *see* Denise

Dolly (Old English) a doll

Dolores (Spanish) lady of sorrow
Also Delora, Delores, Deloris, Delorita, Doloritas, Dolour, Lola, Lolita

Dominique (French) from the Latin for 'belonging to the Lord'
Feminine form of Dominic
Also Domeneca, Domenica, Dominga, Domini, Dominica, Dominik

Donalee (Celtic) sheltered gift

Doncella (Latin) a damsel

Dongala (Old Irish) dark maiden

Donna (Italian) refined lady
Also Dona

Dora *see* Dorothy

Dorcas (Greek) gazelle
Also Dorcea, Dorcia

Doreen (French) the golden or gilded
Also Doireen, Dorene, Dori, Dorie, Dorine, Dory

Dorinda (Greek) the beautiful; of the ocean
Also Dorea, Doria, Dorie, Doris, Dorise, Dorita, Dorris

Doris *see* Dorinda

Dorothy (Greek) gift of God
Also Darata, Darinka, Diorbhail, Dora, Dorchen, Dore, Doretta, Dorosia, Dorota, Dorotea, Doroteja, Dorothea, Dorothee, Dorothi, Dorotka, Dortha, Dorthea, Dorthy, Thea, Theodora
See also Theodora

Dousabel (Old English) sweet and fair
Also Dowsabel
See also Dulcie

Drusilla (Latin) the strong one

Dulcie (Latin) sweet and charming
Diminutive form of Dulcinea
Also Delcine, Dulce, Dulcea, Dulcia, Dulciana, Dulcibella, Dulcibelle, Dulcinea, Dulcinia, Dulcyna

Duvessa (Irish) dark beauty

Dyan *see* Diana

Dymphna (Irish) a poet

Dysis (Greek) the sunset

E

Eartha (Old English) of the earth
Also Ertha

Easter (Old English) from the Germanic goddess of spring

Ebba (Old English) tide

Eden (Hebrew) pleasure or place of pleasure

Edith (Old English) rich, prosperous and happy
Also Eadith, Eaditha, Eda, Edda, Eddeva, Ede, Edetta, Edeva, Edina, Edita, Editha, Edithe, Edyth, Edytha, Edythe

Edmonda (Old English) prosperous protector
Feminine form of Edmund
Also Edmee

Edna (Hebrew) rejuvenation

Edrena (Old English) prosperous ruler
Also Edrea, Edris

Edwina (Old English) rich or happy friend
Feminine form of Edwin
Also Edwinna

Eereena *see* Irene

Effie *see* Euphemia

Eileen (Irish) *see* Helen

Eithne *see* Aithne

Elaine (French) *see* Helen

Elana (Greek) *see* Helen

Elcy (Old German) noble cheer

Eleanor (Provençal) *see* Helen

Electra (Greek) the brilliant one

Elfleda (Old English) noble, beautiful; elf strength
Also Ethelfleda

Elfrida (Old German) wise and peaceful; elfin
Also Elfreda, Elfredah

Elia (Hebrew) God's own

Elisa (German) *see* Elizabeth

Elissa (Phoenician) *see* Elizabeth

Eliza (English) *see* Elizabeth

Elizabeth (Hebrew) oath of God
Also Alzbieta, Alzebeta, Belita, Bess, Besse, Bessie, Bessy, Beth, Betje, Betsy, Bette, Betti, Bettina, Bettisa, Betty, Betuska, Ealasaid, Eilis, Elas, Elen, Elined, Elinud, Elisa, Elisabet, Elisabeth, Elisabetta, Elise, Elissa, Eliza, Ellen, Ellyn, Elsabet, Elsbetchen, Elsbeth, Else, Elsie, Elspeth, Elyssa, Elze, Erzebet, Eylse, Isabeau,

Isabel, Isabella, Isabelle,
Iseabal, Isobel, Liese, Liesel,
Liesl, Lilibet, Lisa, Lisabetta,
Lisabette, Lisette, Liza,
Lizabeth, Lizaveta, Lizette,
Yelisaveta, Ysabel

Ella (Old English) beautiful fairy
maiden
See also Helen

Ellen *see* Elizabeth *and* Helen

Ellora (Greek) happy

Elmira (Old English) of noble
fame
See also Almira

Eloise (Old German) *see*
Louise

Elsa (Old German) *see* Ailsa

Elsie *see* Elizabeth

Elspeth (Scottish) *see*
Elizabeth

Elva (Old German) elfin

Elvira (Latin) white
Also Albina, Albinia, Alvira,
Elvire

Elysia (Greek) pleasure and
happiness

Emerant (Old German) the
emerald

Emily (English) industrious
Also Aimil, Amala, Amalea,
Amalia, Amalie, Amelia,
Amelie, Amelija, Amelina,
Amelinda, Ameline, Amelita,
Amilia, Emalia, Emelda,

Emelia, Emeline, Emera,
Emilia, Emiliana, Emilie,
Emilija, Emlyn, Emmarine,
Emmelina, Emmeline

Emma (Old German) whole or
universal
Also Emme, Emmot, Imma
See also Emily (Emmeline)

Emmanuella (French) from the
Hebrew for 'God is with us'
Feminine form of Emmanuel
See also Manuela

Emmeline *see* Emily

Emogene *see* Imogen

Ena (Gaelic) ardent or fiery

Enid (Celtic) purity of the
soul
Also Enaid

Enola (North American Indian)
alone

Eolande (Greek) born of the
wind

Epifania *see* Tiffany

Eranthe (Greek) alternative
name for the herb camomile

Erica (Old Norse) powerful
ruler
Feminine form of Eric
Also Erika

Erin (Old Irish) girl
Also Erina, Erine, Erinna,
Erinne

Erma *see* Irma

Ermina (Latin) lordly

Ernestine (Old German) earnest
Feminine form of Ernest
Also Erna, Ernesta, Ernestina,
Ernestyna

Ersilia (Gaelic) of Irish
extraction

Esmé *see* Amy

Esmerelda (Spanish) jewel,
emerald
Also Emerald, Esma,
Esmeralda, Esmerolda

Esperance (French) hope

Essie *see* Esther

Estelle (French) *see* Esther

Esther (Persian) a star
Also Eister, Essie, Estella,
Estelle, Estelline, Ester,
Estrelda, Estrella, Estrellita,
Hester, Hestera, Hesther,
Hestia, Hetty, Stella, Stelle

Ethel (Old English) noble
maiden
Also Ethelda, Etheldrid,
Ethelind, Ethelinda, Etheline,
Ethelyn, Ethyle

Etta *see* Henrietta

Ettienette *see* Stephanie

Eucaria (Italian) ready hand,
dextrous
Also Euchira

Eugenia (Greek) nobility,
excellence
Feminine form of Eugene
Also Eugenie, Genie

Eulalia (Greek) of fair speech
Also Eulalie

Eunice (Greek) happy victory

Euphemia (Greek) of good
repute
Also Effie, Eufamie, Eufemia,
Euphemiah, Euphemie,
Euthemie, Phemia

Euphrasia (Greek) generous
and joyful
Also Eufrazya, Euphrazya

Eustacia (Greek) fruitful
Feminine form of Eustace
Also Eustachia, Eustacie,
Stacie, Stacy

Evangeline (French) happy
messenger

Eve (Hebrew) life-giving
Also Aoiffe, Eeva, Eva, Evita,
Evva

Evelyn (Old German) ancestor,
little Eve
Also Evaleen, Evalina,
Eveleen, Evelina, Eveline,
Evlyn

Evonne *see* Yvonne

F

Fabia (Latin) ancient Roman
family name derived from
bean grower
Feminine form of Fabian
Also Fabian, Fabiana,
Fabienne, Fabiola, Fabyan

Faiga (Old English) beautiful

Faine (Old English) joyous
Also Faina, Fayna, Fayne

Fairlee (Old English) beautiful
forest
Also Fairlie

Faith (Latin) to trust
Also Fae, Fay, Faye

Fanny *see* Frances

Far (Chinese) flower

Fay (Old French) *see* Faith

Fayar (Polynesian) dawn

Fayme (Old English) fame
Also Fameuse

Fayola (African) walks with
honour

Fedora *see* Theodora

Felicity (Latin) happy
Feminine form of Felix
Also Felice, Felicia, Felicianna,
Felicidad, Felicie, Felicija,
Felicita, Felicitas, Felicite,
Felicitia, Felis, Felise

Fenella (Gaelic) *see* Fiona

Fern (Old English) a wing or
feather
Also Ferna, Fernas

Fidella (Latin) faithful
Feminine form of Fidel
Also Fedellas, Fidela, Fidelia,
Fidelle, Fidellia, Fidellis

Fifine (Hebrew) addition
Also Fifi

Finella (Celtic) *see* Fiona

Fiona (Gaelic) fair one or white
one
Also Fenella, Fia, Finella, Finola,
Finvola, Fionna, Fionnuala,
Fionnula, Fionola, Fynvola,
Phia, Phio, Phiona, Phionna

Fiorella *see* Florence

Flavia (Latin) blonde or golden-
haired
Also Flavie

Fleur (French) flower
Also Fleurette

Flora (Latin) name of the
goddess of flowers

Florence (Latin) flowering,
flourishing
Also Fiora, Fiorella, Fiorenza,
Firenze, Flora, Flore, Florene,

Florentia, Florentina,
Florentine, Florentyna,
Florenz, Florette, Floria,
Florice, Florinda, Florine,
Floris

Frances (Latin) free; from
France
Feminine form of Francis
Also Fania, Fanny, Fanya, Fraka,
Fran, Franca, Francelia,
Francella, Francesca,
Franchon, Francine, Francisca,
Francisquita, Francoise,
Francyne, Franka, Franzchen,
Franziska, Frasquita

Freda (German) peaceful
Also Frieda, Frida

Frederika (German) peaceful
ruler
Feminine form of Frederick
Also Farica, Fiedricke,
Frederica, Fredericka,
Frederique, Fredrica, Fredrika,
Frenderica, Fridrada

Freya (Old Norse) name of
the goddess of love and
beauty
Also Frea, Freyja

Fuiju (Japanese) winter

Fung (Chinese) bird

G

Gabrielle (Hebrew) woman of God
  Also Gabella, Gable, Gabriel, Gabriela, Gabriella, Gabrilla, Gabrioletta, Gabryela, Gavilla, Gavra

Gaea (Greek) of the earth
  Also Gaia

Gaeta (Sanskrit) holy
  Also Geeta, Gita

Gai (Old French) lively
  Also Gay, Gaye

Gail (Old English) to sing
  Also Gailene, Gale, Gayle, Gaylene
  See also Abigail

Galatea (Greek) milk-white

Garda (Old German) guarded or prepared
  Also Gardas, Gardda, Garde, Gardia
  See also Gertrude

Gay *see* Gai

Gayle *see* Gail

Gaynor *see* Genevieve

Gemma (Latin) precious stone or trinket
  Also Gemmie, Gemsie, Jemma

Genevieve (Celtic) white wave
  Also Ganor, Gaynor, Geneva, Genevieffa, Genevion, Genevra, Gennifer, Genoveva, Genowefa, Ginette, Ginevra, Ginevre, Jenavive, Jennavah, Jennifer, Vanora
  See also Guinevere, Gwendolen

Genie *see* Eugenia

Gentian (Greek) flower name

Georgina (Greek) tiller of the soil
  Feminine form of George
  Also Georgana, Georgene, Georgetta, Georgette, Georgia, Georgiana, Georgienne, Georgine, Gina, Girogia

Geraldine (Old German) spear and rule
  Feminine form of Gerald
  Also Geralda, Geraldina, Gerardine, Gerelda, Gerhardine, Gerlinda, Giralda, Jeraldine

Gerda (Norse) *see* Gertrude

Geremia *see* Jeremia

Germaine (French) of Germany
  Also Germain

Gertrude (Old German) the strong spear-maiden
Also Geltruda, Gerda, Gerde, Gerite, Gerta, Gertrud, Gertrudis, Gerty, Kerttu, Truda, Trude, Trudi, Trudy

Gigi *see* Gilberta

Gilberta (Old German) bright pledge
Feminine form of Gilbert
Also Gigi, Gilberte, Gilbertina, Gilbertine, Wilba, Wilbera, Wilberta

Gilda (Old English) the gilded or golden

Gillian (Latin) young nestling
Also Gileta, Giliana, Giliane, Gill, Gilliet, Gilliette, Jiliette, Jill, Jillian, Jilliana, Jillianne, Jilliette

Gina *see* Georgina

Giselle (Old German) pledge
Also Gisela, Giselda, Gisele, Gisella, Gizela

Githa (Norse) war

Giulia *see* Julia

Gladys (Latin) a sword
Also Gladine, Gladusa, Gladuse, Gwladys

Glenna (Celtic) of the glen or valley
Feminine form of Glen
Also Glenda, Glendene, Glendora, Glenn, Glennie, Glennis, Glenyss, Glynis

Gloria (Latin) glory
Also Gloriana, Gloriane

Glynis *see* Glenna

Godiva (Old English) God's gift

Goldie (Old English) pure gold
Also Golda, Goldea, Goldye, Zlota

Grace (Latin) the loved, favoured, honoured
Also Engracia, Giorsal, Graca, Graciana, Gracie, Gracienne, Graciosa, Gracye, Gratia, Gratiana, Grazia, Graziella, Grazielle, Graziosa, Grecia, Gricia

Gracilia (Latin) slender

Greta (German) *see* Margaret

Gretchen (German) *see* Margaret

Griselda (Old German) grey battle-maid
Also Chriselda, Grisel, Griseldis, Grishilda, Grishilde, Grissell, Grizel, Grizelda, Grizzel, Selda, Zelda

Gudrid (Old Norse) divine passion
Also Gudron, Gudrun, Gudruna, Guthrun

Guida (Italian) perhaps from the Old German for 'wood' or 'a guide'
Feminine form of Guy

Also Guietta, Guillena
Guinevere (Celtic) white
phantom
Also Genevra, Ginevra,
Guenevere, Guinievre
See also Genevieve,
Gwendolen
Gunhild (Old German) brave
warrior-maid
Also Gunhilda, Gunhilde
Gwenda *see* Gwendolen

Gwendolen (Welsh) the white
one
Also Guendolen, Gwen,
Gwenda, Gwendaline,
Gwendolin, Gwendoline,
Gwendolyn, Gwenn
See also Genevieve,
Guinevere
Gwynne *see* Gwyneth
Gwyneth (Welsh) blessed
Also Gwenith, Gwyn, Gwynne,
Venetia

H

Hadassah (Hebrew) a star
  See also Esther
Haidee (Greek) modest,
  caressed
  Also Haida, Haido, Haydee
Halina *see* Helen
Halona (North American
  Indian) happy fortune
  Also Halonna
Hana (Japanese) flower
Hannah (Hebrew) *see* Anne
Harriet (English) home
  ruler
  Feminine form of Harold
  (Harry)
  Also Arriet, Harriett, Harietta,
  Harriette, Harriot, Hatty
  See also Henrietta
Haru (Japanese) spring
Hasina (African) good
Hatty *see* Harriet
Hayley (Old English) hay
  maiden
  Also Haylea, Haylee
Hazel (Old English) the hazel
  tree
Heather (Scottish) flower of the
  moors
Hebe (Greek) youth

Hedda (Old German) war or
  strife
  Also Avice, Avise, Havoise,
  Heda, Hedwig, Hedwiga
  See also Heidi
Heidi (German) battle-maid
  Also Heide, Heidy, Hidie
Helen (Greek) bright one
  Also Aileen, Ailienor, Alaine,
  Alaune, Alena, Alene, Alienor,
  Aline, Eileen, Eilene, Eilleen,
  Elain, Elaine, Elana, Elayne,
  Eleanor, Eleanora, Eleanore,
  Eleen, Elena, Elene, Elenor,
  Elenore, Eleonore, Elidh, Elini,
  Elinor, Elinore, Elionor, Ellen,
  Ellene, Ellenis, Ellette, Ellie,
  Ellin, Ellyn, Elmor, Elna,
  Elnore, Elyn, Gailina, Galena,
  Galina, Halina, Helaine,
  Helena, Helene, Helenka,
  Helenora, Hellene, Ileana,
  Ilene, Illene, Ilona, Jelena,
  Jeleta, Jellica, Laine, Lana,
  Lani, Leanor, Lena, Lenia,
  Lenke, Lenni, Lennie, Lenor,
  Lenore, Leonora, Leonore,
  Leora, Lora, Lorene, Lorine,
  Narelle, Nell, Nella, Nellette,

Nelliana, Nellie, Nillette, Nora, Norah, Norelle, Yelena

Helga (Old Norse) the holy
Also Elga, Olga

Helise (Greek) of the Elysian fields
Also Helice

Heloise (French) *see* Louise

Henrietta (Old German) home ruler
Feminine form of Henry
Also Eiric, Enrica, Enrichetta, Enrieta, Enrika, Enriqueta, Enriquette, Etta, Hattie, Hendrica, Hendrika, Henka, Henrieta, Henriette, Henrika, Henrike, Henriqueta, Jettchen, Jindriska, Nettie
See also Harriet, Yetta

Hepzibah (Hebrew) my delight is in her
Also Hebzi, Hebzibeth, Hephzibah, Hephzipa, Hepsiba, Hepsibah, Hepsy, Hepza, Zipah

Hera (Greek) queen of the gods and protector of women

Hermione (Greek) noble
Feminine form of Hermes
Also Hermanda, Hermandine, Hermia, Hermine, Herminia, Irma

Hester *see* Esther

Hilary (Greek) cheerful and merry
Also Hilar, Hilaria, Hillari

Hilda (Old English) battle
Also Hilde, Hildie, Hiltrud, Hylda, Ilda, Ilde

Hildegarde (Old German) protecting battle-maid
Also Hildagard, Hildagarde, Hildegard
See also Hilda

Hippolyta (Greek) liberator of horses
Feminine form of Hippolytus

Hiroko (Japanese) generous

Holly (Old English) holy
Also Hollie

Honey (Old English) sweet one

Hong (Chinese) pink

Honora (Latin) reputation for beauty
Also Annora, Honora, Honoria, Nora, Norah, Onora, Onoria

Hope (Old English) to hope or cherish
See also Nadia

Hortense (Latin) a lady gardener
Also Hortencia, Hortensa, Hortensia, Hortenzia, Ortensa, Ortensia

Hoshi (Japanese) star

Howin (Chinese) a loyal swallow

Hua (Chinese) flower, blossom
Hulda (Norse) muffled or
  covered
Huli (Chinese) fox spirit
Hyacinth (Greek) flower name
  or colour purple

Also Chinta, Giacinta,
Hyacintha, Hyacinthia,
Hyacinthies, Jacinda,
Jacinta, Jacintha, Jacinthe,
Jacyne
Hypatia (Greek) superior

I

Ianthe (Greek) *see* Violet

Ida (Old German) happy
Also Idaka, Idalia, Idda, Idetta, Idette

Idala (Hebrew) one who goes softly

Idona (Old Norse) name of the goddess of spring
Also Edony, Idonea, Idonia

Ignacia (Latin) ardent; fiery
Feminine form of Ignatius
Also Igna, Ignazia, Ignezia, Iniga

Ila (French) isle

Ilka (Scottish) each and every one
(Slavonic) flattering
Also Milka

Ilona (Hungarian) *see* Helen

Ilsa *see* Ailsa

Imelda *see* Imogen

Imogen (Latin) image of her mother
Also Emogene, Imagina, Imelda, Imogene, Imogine, Imojean

Ina (Filipino) mother

Inari (Japanese) keeper of rice

Indira (Sanskrit) an Indian goddess

Indra (Hindustani) the thunder
Also Indred

Inez (Spanish) *see* Agnes

Ingrid (Old Norse) the daughter of the great hero Ing
Also Inga, Ingar, Inge, Ingeberg, Inger, Ingria, Ingrida, Ingunna

Inocenta (Italian) innocent
Also Chencho, Innocenty

Iola (Greek) dawn cloud
Also Iole

Iolanthe (Greek) *see* Violet

Irene (Greek) peace
Also Arina, Eereena, Eereenia, Eirena, Eirene, Erena, Irena, Irenka, Irina

Iris (Greek) the rainbow

Irma (Old German) strong
(Latin) noble person
Also Erma, Ermina, Erminia, Irme, Irmina, Irmine
See also Hermione

Iruka (African) the future is supreme

Isa (Old German) iron-like

Isadora (Greek) the gift of Isis
Feminine form of Isidore
Also Dora, Isadore, Isidora

Ismenia (Greek) learned
Also Ismena
Isobel *see* Elizabeth
Isolda (Old German) ice rule
Also Isolde

Ita (Gaelic) desire for truth
Ivy (Old English) ivy vine
Also Ivana, Ive, Ivis

J

Jacinta *see* Hyacinth

Jacobina (Scottish) *see* Jacqueline

Jacqueline (French) from the Hebrew for 'the supplanter' Feminine form of Jacob (Jacques)
Also Jacalyn, Jacina, Jackelyn, Jacoba, Jacobee, Jacobella, Jacobina, Jacobine, Jacomina, Jacovina, Jacquelina, Jacquelyn, Jacquenella, Jacquenetta, Jacquenette, Jacquetta, Jacquette, Jacqui, Jakolin, Jakolina, Zakolina
See also Jamesina

Jade (Chinese) love

Jama (Sanskrit) daughter

Jamesina (Scottish) from the Hebrew for 'the supplanter' Feminine form of Jacob (James)
Also Jesma
See also Jacqueline

Jamila (Arabic) beautiful

Jan *see* Jane

Jana *see* Jane

Jane (Hebrew) God is gracious Feminine form of John
Also Gian, Gianina, Gianna, Giovanna, Ivanka, Jan, Jana, Janeen, Janeis, Janel, Janella, Janelle, Janelyn, Janet, Janeta, Janeth, Janetta, Janette, Janica, Janice, Janie, Janina, Janine, Janis, Janka, Jann, Janna, Jannah, Janne, Jasia, Jayne, Jean, Jeanette, Jeanine, Jeanne, Jehanne, Jenet, Jenka, Jennetta, Jennette, Jhone, Joan, Joana, Joanie, Joanna, Joanne, Johanna, Jone, Joni, Jonie, Jonita, Jovanna, Juana, Juanita, Seonaid, Shane, Shauna, Sheena, Sheenah, Sheenaugh, Shena, Shene, Shona, Sian, Sine, Sinead, Siobhan, Zane, Zaneta

Janelle *see* Jane

Janice *see* Jane

Janina (Sanskrit) the kind
See also Jane

Jarita (Hindustani) the bird
Also Arita, Gerita, Jerita, Rita

Jarvia (Old German) sharp as a spear Feminine form of Jarvis

Jasmine (Persian) the jasmine flower
Also Jamina, Jasmin, Jasmina, Jassamine, Jessamine, Jessamy, Jessamyn, Yasmin, Yasmine

Javana (Sanskrit) swift, fleet

Jayne *see* Jane

Jean (Scottish) *see* Jane

Jeanette (French) *see* Jane

Jemima (Hebrew) the dove, the symbol of peace
Also Jemena, Jemimah, Jemina, Jeminah, Jeminine

Jemma *see* Gemma

Jennifer (English) *see* Genevieve

Jeremia (Hebrew) the Lord's exalted
Feminine form of Jeremiah
Also Geremia

Jessamine (French) *see* Jasmine

Jessica (Hebrew) God's grace; he beholds
Feminine form of Jesse
Also Jessalyn, Jesseline, Jessie, Jessika, Jesslyn

Jezebel (Hebrew) devotee of Baal, a false god

Jillian *see* Gillian

Joan *see* Jane

Joanna *see* Jane

Jocasta (Greek) queen of Thebes

Jocelyn (Latin) just one
Also Giusta, Giustina, Jocelin, Joceline, Jodoca, Joscelind, Josceline, Joscely, Joscelyn, Joslin, Josselyn, Joycelin

Jocosa (Latin) playful

Jodie *see* Judith

Johanna *see* Jane

Joletta (Latin) *see* Violet

Jolie (French) pretty

Josephine (French) from the Hebrew for 'increaser'
Feminine form of Joseph
Also Giuseppina, Iosefini, Josefa, Josefina, Josepha, Josephe, Josephie, Josephina, Josette, Jozia, Jozka, Juozapina, Pepina, Pepita

Joy (Latin) to rejoice
Also Joice, Joyan, Joyce, Joye, Joyons

Joyce *see* Joy

Juanita (Spanish) *see* Jane

Judith (Hebrew) woman of Judea; a jewess
Also Giuditta, Iudita, Jodi, Jodie, Jody, Judi, Judie, Judita, Juditha, Judithe, Judy, Jutha, Jutta, Jytte, Yudif

Julia (Latin) youthful one
Feminine form of Julian
Also Giulia, Giuliana, Giulietta, Ioula, Iulia, Joletta, Juliana, Juliane, Julianne, Julie,

Julienne, Juliet, Julieta,
Julietta, Juliette, Julija, Julina,
Juline, Julita, Julyan, Zulliette

Jun (Chinese) truth

June (Latin) youth; born in the
month of June
Also Jeno, Juna, Junella,
Juneth, Junette, Junia, Junna,
Junno, Juno

Justine (French) from the Latin
for 'the just'
Feminine form of Justin
Also Guistina, Justa, Justicia,
Justina, Justinka, Yustyna

Juventia (Latin) name of the
goddess of youth

K

Kachina (North American Indian) sacred dancer
Kama (Sanskrit) love
Kamala (Sanskrit) lotus
Kamania (African) like the moon
Kameka (Japanese) long-lived
Kane (Japanese) golden
Karen (Danish) *see* Catherine
Karma (Sanskrit) destiny
  Also Carma
Karoline *see* Caroline
Kasia (Polish) *see* Catherine
Kate *see* Catherine
Katherine *see* Catherine
Kathleen *see* Catherine
Katinka (Russian) *see* Catherine
Katrina *see* Catherine
Kay (Greek) to rejoice
  Also Kaya, Kaye, Kaylene
  See also Catherine
  (Katherine)
Keely (Gaelic) the beautiful one
  Also Keele, Keelie
Keiko (Japanese) beloved, adored
Kelly (Gaelic) warrior-maid
Kelsey (Old Norse) from the island

Kendra (Old English) knowing or understanding
  Also Kenna
Kerry (Celtic) the dark
  Also Keri, Kerrie
Ketura (Hebrew) incense, fragrance
  Also Keturah
Kezia (Hebrew) the cassia tree
  Also Kazia, Kesi, Kesia, Kesiah, Ketsy, Kezi, Kitsy
Kiki (Egyptian) the castor plant
Kim (English) chief or ruler
  Also Kym
  See also Kimberley
Kimberley (English) from the royal meadow
  Also Kimberly
Kineta (Greek) active
Kira (Persian) sun
Kiri (Maori) tree bark
  Also Kirilees, Kirilly, Kirri
Kirsten (Scottish) *see* Christine
Kitty *see* Catherine
Kiyoko (Japanese) clear
Klara (German) *see* Clare
Kora *see* Cora
Krishna (Sanskrit) dark or black

Kuki (Japanese) snow
Kuni (Japanese) country born
Kwai (Chinese) fragrance of a
  rose

Kylie (Aboriginal) boomerang
Kyna (Welsh) wise and mighty
  Feminine form of Conan
  (Kynan)

L

Laelia (Hebrew) devoted to the Lord
  Also Laila, Lela, Lelah, Lelia, Lelie
Lais (Greek) rejoice
  Also Laise
Lakshmi (Sanskrit) success and beauty
Lala (Slavonic) tulip
Lalage (Greek) babble
Lalla (Scottish) of the lowlands
Lana *see* Alana
Lara (Latin) famous, shining
  Also Larah, Larentia, Laretta
Larissa (Greek) cheerful one
Laura (Latin) crowned with laurel
  Feminine form of Laurence
  Also Lari, Laurana, Lauranna, Laure, Laureen, Laurel, Lauren, Laurena, Laurencia, Laurene, Laurentia, Laurentina, Lauretta, Laurette, Laurinda, Lora, Loralie, Lore, Loree, Lorelie, Lorelle, Loren, Lorena, Lorenza, Loretta, Lorette, Lori, Lorinda, Lorine, Loris, Lorita, Lorna, Lorne, Lorrie, Loure, Lourane, Lourena
Laurel *see* Laura
Lauren *see* Laura
Lavinia (Latin) woman of Latium
  Also Laletta
Layla (African) born at night
Lea (English) the lea or grassland
  Also Leigh
Leah (Hebrew) the weary one
Leala (Old French) faithful
Leanne *combination* of Lee and Anne
  See also Liana
Lee (Chinese) plum
Leigh *see* Lea
Leila (Persian) dark, oriental beauty
Leilani (Hawaiian) heavenly blossom
  Also Lillani, Lullani
Lena *see* Helen
Leonie (Latin) the lion
  Feminine form of Leo
  Also Leocadia, Leola, Leona, Leonarda, Leone, Leonella, Leonelle, Leoni, Leonia,

Leonina, Leonine, Leontine,
Leontyne
Leonora *see* Helen (Eleanor)
Lesley (Celtic) from the grey
stronghold
Feminine form of Leslie
Also Leslee, Lesleigh
Letitia (Latin) gladness
Also Laetitia, Lece, Leda,
Leetice, Leticia, Letizia, Letta,
Lettice
Lettice (English) *see* Letitia
Lewanna (Hebrew) as pure as
the white moon
Lian (Chinese) graceful
willow
Liana (French) to bind
See also Leanne
Lida (Slavonic) loved by all
people
Liesl (German) *see* Elizabeth
Lila *see* Delilah
Lilac (Persian) blue; flower
name
Lilith (Assyrian) storm demon
Lillian (Latin) flower name, lily
Also Lela, Lelah, Lelia, Lila,
Lilah, Lili, Lilia, Lilian, Liliana,
Liliane, Lilianna, Liliarna,
Lilias, Lilicia, Lilja, Liljana,
Lillah, Lillis, Lily, Lilyan
Linda (Old German) wise
serpent
Also Linde, Lindi, Lindie,

Lindy, Lynd, Lynda, Lynn,
Lynne
See also Belinda, Melinda
Linette *see* Lynette
Lisa *see* Elizabeth
Lisette *see* Elizabeth
Lisle (Old English) of the island
Lissabelle (Latin) beautiful
honey bee
Liza *see* Elizabeth
Lois (Greek) free to please
Lola (Spanish) *see* Charlotte,
Dolores
Lorelei (German) lurer to the
rock
Loretta *see* Laura
Lori *see* Laura
Loris *see* Chloris
Lorna (Celtic) name of a
goddess of the moors
See also Laura
Lorraine (French) famous in
battle
Also Laraine, Loraine
Louise (Latin) to hear and to
fight
Feminine form of Lewis (Louis)
Also Aloisa, Aloisia, Aloyse,
Eloisa, Eloise, Heloisa,
Heloise, Labhaoise, Loise,
Louisa, Louisetta, Louisette,
Lovisa, Loyce, Ludvika,
Luigia, Luisa, Luise, Lujza,
Lujzka, Lula

Lucasta *see* Lucy
Lucia (Italian) *see* Lucy
Lucinda *see* Lucy
Lucretia (Latin) riches or
   reward
   Feminine form of Lucretius
   Also Lucrece, Lucrecia,
   Lucree, Lucrezia
Lucy (Latin) light
   Also Cindy, Lucasta, Lucette,
   Lucia, Luciana, Lucida, Lucie,
   Lucienne, Lucila, Lucile,
   Lucilia, Lucilla, Lucille,
   Lucina, Lucinda, Lucza,
   Luighseach, Luisadh, Luz,
   Luzette, Luzie, Luzija, Luzinde
Luella (Old English) famous elf
   Also Llewella, Louella, Loulle,
   Lovella, Luelle
Lulabel (Old German) beautiful
   war hero

Lulu (African) precious pearl
Lurline (Old German) the
   alluring
Lycia *see* Alice
Lydia (Greek) woman of Lydia,
   a rich trading country in
   ancient Asia Minor
   Also Lidia, Lidie, Lidika, Lydie
Lynda *see* Linda
Lyndal (Old English) in the
   dale
   Also Lindall
Lyndsay (Old English) linden
   tree
   Also Lyndsey
Lynette (Latin) the flax
   Also Eluned, Linetta, Linette,
   Lyneth, Lynetta, Lynette,
   Lynn
Lynn *see* Linda, Lynette
Lysandra (Greek) liberator

M

Mab (Celtic) joy

Mabel (Latin) lovable
Also Amabel, Amabella,
Annabel, Annabella, Arrabel,
Arrabella, Mabella, Mabelle,
Mabilia, Mabilla, Mable,
Maible, Mas, Maybelle

Madeline (Hebrew) woman of
Magdala in Galilee
Also Madalene, Madaline,
Madalon, Madalyn,
Maddalena, Maddie, Madel,
Madelaine, Madeleine,
Madelena, Madelene,
Madelina, Madella, Madelle,
Madelon, Madlen, Madlena,
Madlin, Madlyn, Mady, Magda,
Magdala, Magdalen,
Magdalena, Magdalene,
Magdaline, Magdolna,
Maighdlin, Malena, Malina,
Marlane, Marlene, Marleen,
Marlina, Marline

Madge *see* Margaret

Madhura (Sanskrit) charming,
delightful

Maeve (Celtic) intoxicating
joy
Also Mave, Meave

Magda (German) *see* Madeline

Magnolia (French) flower
named after botanist Pierre
Magnol

Mahlah (Hebrew) mild

Maida (Old English) the maiden
Also Maidel, Maidie, Mayda,
Mayde, Maydena

Maire (Irish) *see* Mary

Maisie (Scottish) *see* Margaret

Makaira (Japanese) happy

Mali *see* Malvina

Malina (Danish) *see* Madeline

Malvina (Old German) smooth
brow
Feminine form of Melvin
Also Maleena, Mali, Malin,
Mallie, Mallina, Malva,
Malvinia, Mellie, Melvina,
Melvine, Molina

Mame *see* Mary

Manuela (Spanish) God with
us
Feminine form of Manuel
Also Manella, Mannuela,
Manuelita, Uella
See also Emmanuella

Mara *see* Mary

Marcella *see* Marcia

Marcia (Latin) belonging to
Mars, the god of war
Feminine form of Mark
Also Marcela, Marcelia,
Marcelina, Marcelinda,
Marceline, Marcella, Marcelle,
Marcellina, Marcelline,
Marcerita, Marcheta,
Marchita, Marciana, Marcie,
Marcille, Marcine, Marcite,
Marka, Marquita, Marsha

Mardi (French) Tuesday

Margaret (Latin) pearl
Also Greta, Gretchen, Gretel,
Madge, Madlinka, Mairghread,
Maisie, Marcail, Margareta,
Margarete, Margaretha,
Margaretta, Margarida,
Margarita, Margaux, Margelo,
Margery, Marget, Margette,
Margharita, Margherethe,
Margherita, Margory, Margot,
Margred, Margret, Marguerita,
Marguerite, Marjorie, Marjory,
Marret, May, Maygan,
Meadleh, Meagan, Meaghan,
Meg, Megan, Meghann, Meta,
Peg, Peggy
See also Rita

Margery (English) *see* Margaret

Margherita (Spanish) *see*
Margaret and Rita

Margita (Sanskrit) sought after

Margot (French) *see* Margaret

Maria (Latin) *see* Mary

Marian *see* Mary

Maribelle *combination* of Mary
and Belle
Also Marabelle, Maribel,
Maribella, Marybelle

Marie (French) *see* Mary

Marietta (American) *see* Mary

Marigold (English) flower name

Marika (Spanish) *see* Mary

Marilyn (American) *see* Mary

Marina (Latin) of the sea
Also Mareena, Marisa

Marion (English) *see* Mary

Marjorie *see* Margaret

Marlene (Hebrew) the elevated
See also Madeline

Marsha *see* Marcia

Martha (Aramaic) head of the
household
Also Marta, Martel, Martella,
Marthe, Marthena, Marti,
Martita, Mattie, Matty,
Moireach

Martina (Latin) after Mars, the
god of war
Feminine form of Martin
Also Martine, Tina

Mary (Hebrew) bitterness
Also Mair, Maire, Mame,
Mamie, Manette, Manon, Mara,
Marea, Marella, Maretta,
Marette, Mari, Maria, Mariam,
Mariamne, Marian, Mariana,

Marianna, Marianne, Marica,
Marie, Mariel, Mariet, Marietje,
Marietta, Mariette, Marika,
Marilin, Marilla, Marilyn,
Marion, Marionette, Mariquita,
Marita, Mariya, Marja, Marla,
Marya, Maryanne, Marylin,
Marylon, Marylyn, Maryon,
Maryse, Marysia, Masha,
Maura, Maureen, Maurizia,
May, Mearr, Mija, Miriam,
Mitzi, Mo, Moira, Moire, Molly,
Moreena, Morena, Moya,
Moyra, Muire, Polly

Marylou *combination* of Mary
and Louise

Mary-Rose *combination* of
Mary and Rose

Matilda (Old German) mighty
and strong battle-maid
Also Maitilde, Matelda,
Mathilda, Mathilde, Matilde,
Maud, Maude, Tilly

Matsu (Japanese) happy

Maude *see* Matilda

Maureen (Irish) *see* Mary

Mavis (Old French) the song
thrush
Also Mavas

Maxine (French) the greatest
Feminine form of Maximilian
Also Maxima, Maxime

May (Latin) of the month of May
See also Mary

Maya (Sanskrit) art and wisdom

Megan (Welsh) *see* Margaret

Melaine *see* Melanie

Melanie (Greek) dark or black
Also Melaina, Melaine,
Melania, Melantha, Melany,
Melena, Melloney, Mellony,
Melony

Melba (Old English) from the
mill stream
Feminine form of Melbourne

Melina *see* Carmel and Melinda

Melinda (Greek) mild and
gentle
Also Malinda, Malinde, Melina,
Melynda
See also Linda

Melissa (Greek) honey or
honey-bee
Also Elita, Malita, Melessa,
Melice, Melisma, Melisse,
Melita, Melitta, Melleta, Mellie,
Mellita, Milice, Millissa, Missi

Melody (Greek) a song

Mercy (Latin) compassion
Also Mena, Mercedes

Meredith (Celtic) protector of
the sea

Merryn (English) wave of the
sea
Also Merewenna, Meruvina,
Merwin, Morwenna

Meryl (Latin) *see* Muriel

Meta (Latin) ambition or goal

Mia (Italian/Spanish) my own

Michelle (French) from the Hebrew for 'Who is like God?'
Feminine form of Michael
Also Micaela, Mical, Micala, Michaela, Michaele, Michaelina, Michaella, Michel, Michela, Michele, Michelina, Micheline, Michellia, Miguela, Miguelita, Mikaela, Mikala, Miquela

Mignon (French) delicate, dainty
Also Mignonette, Mignonne, Mignot

Mila (Italian) lovable
Also Milo

Mildred (Old English) mild power
Also Mildrid

Millicent (Old German) strong or energetic worker
Also Melesina, Melicent, Melisande, Mellicent, Melusine, Milicent, Milisent, Millisent

Mimi *see* Minette

Minerva (Latin) mind, remember; name of the Roman goddess of wisdom

Minette (Old German) resolute antagonist
Also Mimi

Minna (Old German) loving memory

Mirabel (Latin) admired for her beauty
Also Marabel, Mirabella, Mirabelle, Mirella

Miranda (Latin) worthy to be admired

Miriam *see* Mary
Also Miriamme

Mitzi *see* Mary

Moira (Irish) *see* Mary

Molly (Irish) *see* Mary

Mona (Irish) noble
Also Moyna

Monica (Latin) adviser
Also Monicia, Monika, Monike, Monique

Monique (French) *see* Monica

Morag (Gaelic) sun
See also Sarah

Morgan (Welsh) from the sea
Also Morgaine, Morgana

Morna (Gaelic) beloved
Also Myrna

Morwenna *see* Merryn

Moto (Japanese) source

Muriel (Greek) myrrh, perfume
Also Merl, Merle, Merlina, Merline, Merola, Merrill, Merrilla, Meryl, Muirgheal, Murial, Murieall, Murielle, Myrlene

Musetta (Old French) quiet
  pastoral song
Myfanwy (Welsh) my fine
  one
  Also Miffany, Myvanwy

Myra (Greek) she who weeps or
  laments
  Also Mira
Myrtle (Greek) plant name
  Also Myrtilla

N

Nadia (Russian) hope
  Also Nada, Nadine, Nadejda
Nadine *see* Nadia
Nami (Japanese) wave
Nancy *see* Anne
Nannette (French) *see* Anne
  (Hannah)
Naomi (Hebrew) pleasant
  one
  Also Naoma, Noami, Nomi
Nara (Old Norse) nearest to
Narcissa (Greek) self-
  worshipping
Narelle *see* Helen
  Also Norelle
Nastasya (Russian) *see*
  Anastasia
Nata (Sanskrit) dancer
Natalie (Latin) natal or birth
  day
  Also Natala, Natale, Natalia,
  Nataline, Natalka, Natasha,
  Nathalia, Nathalie, Natica,
  Natika
  See also Noeline
Natasha (Russian) *see* Natalie
Natsu (Japanese) summer
Nefertiti (Egyptian) the
  beautiful one has come

Nelda (Old English) elder
  tree
Nella *see* Helen
Neoma (Greek) the new
  moon
  Also Neomah
Nerilee *see* Nerolie
Nerine (Latin) of the sea
  Also Nerice, Nerissa, Nerita
Nerolie (Italian) the black
  Feminine form of Nero
  Also Nerilee
Nesta (Welsh) *see* Agnes
Netta (Latin) pure and neat
  See also Antonia (Antoinette),
  Henrietta, Jane (Jeanette)
Neysa *see* Agnes
Nicole (Greek) the people's
  victory
  Feminine form of Nicholas
  Also Coletta, Colette, Collette,
  Nichola, Nicola, Nicoletta,
  Nicolette, Nicolina, Nicoline
Nidra (Sanskrit) sleep
Nina (Russian) *see* Anne
  (Annina)
Nissa (Scandinavian) friendly
  elf; fairy who can only be seen
  by lovers

Noeline (Old German) *see* Noelle

Noelle (French) Christmas Feminine form of Noel
Also Noelie, Noelita, Noella, Noeline

Nola (Celtic) the noble

Nona (Latin) the ninth child
Also Nonie

Nora (Irish) *see* Helen (Eleanor), Honora

Norma (Latin) the norm, rule or pattern

Nuala (Irish) fair-shouldered

O

Obelia (Greek) from obelisk (pillar)

Octavia (Latin) the eighth child
Feminine form of Octavius
Also Octavie, Oktavija, Ottavia, Tavia

Odessa (Greek) of the Odyssey

Odette (French) home lover
Also Odala, Odelia, Odella, Odila, Odilla, Odille, Othilia, Otila, Ottilia

Olga (Old German) *see* Helga

Olivia (Latin) the olive tree, symbol of peace
Feminine form of Oliver
Also Olive, Olivette, Olva

Olwen (Welsh) white footprint, clover
Also Olwyn

Olympia (Greek) of Olympus, the home of the gods
Also Olimpia, Olimpias, Olympe, Olympias, Olympie, Pia

Ona/Oona (Lithuanian) *see* Una

Ondine (Latin) *see* Undine

Oneida (North American Indian) the awaited or expected

Opal (Sanskrit) precious stone, jewel

Ophelia (Greek) a serpent; invincible and wise
Also Ofelia, Ofeliga, Ofilia, Ophelie, Phelia

Ora *see* Aurora

Oralia *see* Oriel

Oriana (Latin) the dawning
Also Oriande, Oriante

Oriel (English) a window
Also Oralia

Orlanda (Italian) *see* Rolanda

Orsa/Orsola *see* Ursula

P

Pagan (Latin) villager

Page (English) attendant
 Also Paige

Paloma (Spanish) the dove

Pamela (Greek) sweetness
 Also Pamelina, Pamella,
 Pamsin

Pandora (Greek) gifted

Pansofia (Greek) all wisdom
 See also Sophia

Pansy (French) thought;
 fragrant flower

Panya (African) a twin child

Paola see Paula

Pascha (Middle English) Easter
 child
 Also Paschale, Pasquette

Patience (Latin) endurance

Patricia (Latin) noble, well-
 born
 Feminine form of Patrick
 Also Patreeza, Patrice,
 Patrizia, Patsy

Paula (Latin) small
 Feminine form of Paul
 Also Paola, Paolina, Paule,
 Paulette, Paulina, Pauline,
 Paulita, Pavia, Pavla, Pavlica

Pauline see Paula

Pavla (Czechoslovakian) see
 Paula

Pazanne (French) country
 woman
 Also Pezaine

Pearl (Latin) a jewel
 Also Pearla, Perle

Peg see Margaret

Penelope (Greek) uncertain
 origin; symbol of wifely
 fidelity
 Also Pennie, Penny

Perdita (Latin) lost

Perizada (Persian) fairy-born

Persis (Greek) Persian woman

Peta see Petra

Petra (Greek) stone or rock
 Feminine form of Peter
 Also Parnel, Peita, Perinna,
 Peronella, Perrine, Peta,
 Petrea, Petrina, Petriona,
 Petronella, Petronia,
 Petronilla, Petronille, Pier,
 Pierella, Pierette, Pierina

Petula (Latin) seeker

Petunia (Indian) a flower

Phaedora (Greek) a gift of
 God

Phanessa see Vanessa

Phedra (Greek) bright
 Also Phaedra
Philadelphia (Greek) brotherly
 love
Philippa (Greek) lover of
 horses
 Feminine form of Philip
 Also Felipa, Filippa, Phillipa
Phillida *see* Phyllis
Philomena (Greek) beloved
Phoebe (Greek) goddess of the
 moon
 Also Phebe
Phryne (Greek) pale and delicate
Phyllis (Greek) leafy green
 bough
 Also Fillis, Phillida, Phillyda,
 Phyllida, Phyllys

Pia (Latin) devout
 See also Olympia
Pier *see* Petra
Placida (Latin) calm
Polly *see* Mary
Poppy (Latin) flower
 symbolising peace
Portia (Latin) a harbour,
 safety
Primrose (Latin) the first
 rose
 See also Rose
Priscilla (Latin) the primitive
 or ancient
 Also Cilla, Prisca, Priscella
Prudence (Latin) discretion
 Also Prudencia, Prudentia
Prunella (Latin) little plum

Q

Queenie (English) a pet name for girls called Victoria during the time of that queen's reign
Also Queena, Queeny

Querida (Spanish) beloved

Quintina (Latin) the fifth child
Also Quinta, Quintella, Quintilla

R

Rachel (Hebrew) ewe, symbolising innocence
Also Rachael, Rachela, Rachele, Rachelle, Raechael, Rahel, Raoghnailt, Raquel, Raychela, Shelley
Rae (Scandinavian) a doe
Raina *see* Regina
Ramona (Old German) wise and mighty protector
Feminine form of Raymond
Also Raimonda, Ramonda
Rani (Sanskrit) a royal princess
Raquel *see* Rachel
Rati (Sanskrit) love and desire
Rebecca (Hebrew) compliant wife
Also Rebeca, Rebeccah, Rebeka, Rebekah, Rebekka, Rivkah
Regan *see* Regina
Regina (Latin) queen
Also Raina, Regan, Reina, Reyna
Rei (Japanese) ceremonious
Ren (Japanese) intelligence
Renata (Latin) born again
Also Rena, Renate, Rene, Renee

Renee (French) *see* Renata
Rhea (Greek) poppy; flowering from the earth
Also Rea
Rhian (Welsh) maiden
Rhiannon (Welsh) nymph
Rhoda (Greek) rose
Also Rhodeia, Rhodia
Rhonda (Welsh) after a valley in southern Wales
Rhonwen (Celtic) white skirt
Ria (Spanish) the river
See also Mary (Maria)
Rina (Greek) pure
Riona (Irish) queenly
Rita (Sanskrit) order or law
See also Margaret (Margherita)
Roberta (Old German) bright shining fame
Feminine form of Robert
Also Bobbette, Robena, Robertina, Robin, Robina, Robine, Robinetta, Robinette, Robinia, Robyn, Ruperta
Robyn (Old English) *see* Roberta

Rochelle (Latin) little rock
Feminine form of Roche
Also Rochella, Rochette

Roesia (Old French) *see* Rose

Rohana (Sanskrit) sandalwood tree

Rolanda (Old German) fame of the land
Feminine form of Roland
Also Orlanda

Romola (Latin) fame

Rosa *see* Rose

Rosalie *see* Rose

Rosalind (Old German) *see* Rose

Rosamund (Old German) pure or clean rose
Also Rosamond, Rosamonda, Rosamunda, Rozamond

Rose (Latin) flower name
Also Ralia, Rasche, Roesia, Rohesia, Rosa, Rosabel, Rosabella, Rosalba, Rosaleen, Rosalia, Rosalie, Rosalija, Rosalind, Rosalinda, Rosalinde, Roseanna, Roseanne, Rosel, Roseta, Rosetta, Rosie, Rosina, Rosita, Roslyn, Royce, Royse, Roysia, Rozalind, Rozelle
See also Primrose, Rosemary

Rosemary (Latin) name for herb of remembrance
Also Rose Marie, Rosemare, Rosemari, Rosemarie
See also Rose

Rosetta (French) *see* Rose

Rosina (Italian) *see* Rose

Rosita (Spanish) *see* Rose

Rowena (Celtic) white-maned
Also Renwien, Rhonwen

Roxanna (Persian) brilliant
Also Roschana, Roxana, Roxanne, Roxine

Ruby (English) precious stone

Ruth (Hebrew) kind friend
Also Rutha, Ruthe, Ruthi, Ruthia, Ruthie

S

Sabah (Arabic) morning

Sabina (Italian) woman of Sabine people in ancient Italy
Also Sabin, Sabine, Sabiny, Saidhghin, Savina

Sabrina (Latin) princess

Sacha (Russian) *see* Alexandra

Sachiko (Japanese) joy

Sadie *see* Sarah

Sai (Japanese) intelligence

Salena (Greek) salty
Also Salina

Sally *see* Sarah

Salome (Hebrew) peaceful

Samantha (Aramaic) listener

Sanchia (Spanish) holy
Also Sancha, Sancta, Sancya

Sandra *see* Alexandra (Alessandra), Cassandra

Sapphire (Hebrew) like a sapphire stone, jewel

Sarah (Hebrew) princess
Also Morag, Sade, Sadella, Sadie, Sadye, Saida, Salaidh, Sallie, Sally, Sara, Saraid, Sarene, Saretta, Sarette, Sari, Sarie, Sarine, Sarita, Sarka, Sayda, Sirri, Sorcha, Zaddah, Zahra, Zara, Zarah, Zaras, Zaria

Sarasa (Sanskrit) beautiful, gracious

Scarlett (Old English) a rich red colour

Selena (Greek) name of the moon goddess
Also Celene, Celie, Celina, Celinda, Celine, Selene, Selina, Selinda

Septima (Latin) seventh child

Seraphina (Hebrew) the enthusiastic believer
Also Serafina, Serafine, Seraphia, Seraphine, Seraphita

Serena (Latin) calm, tranquil

Shaina (Yiddish) beautiful

Shane *see* Jane

Shani (African) wonderful

Shannon (Celtic) slow waters

Shantelle *see* Chantal

Sharleen *see* Caroline

Sharon (Hebrew) a princess
Also Sharee, Sharne, Sharolyn

Shauna (Irish) *see* Jane

Sheba *see* Bathsheba

Sheena (English) *see* Jane (Sine)
Also Sheenah, Shena

Sheila (Irish) *see* Cecilia

Shelley (Old English) from the edge of the meadow
See also Rachel

Sheryl *see* Cheryl

Shimona (Hebrew) little princess
Also Mona

Shirley (Old English) the shining meadow
Also Shirlea, Shirlee, Shirleen, Shirlene, Shirlie

Shona (Celtic) *see* Jane

Sibil *see* Sybil

Sidra (Latin) of the stars

Sigrid (Old Norse) victory ride

Silvana *see* Sylvia
Also Silvaine

Simone (Hebrew) one who hears
Feminine form of Simon
Also Simona, Simonetta, Simonette, Simonne

Sine (Scottish) *see* Jane

Sinead (Irish) *see* Jane

Siobhan (Irish) *see* Jane (Joanna)

Sirena (Greek) sweet singer or siren

Sisi (African) born on Sunday

Sita (Sanskrit) furrow

Sofia *see* Sophia

Sondra *see* Alexandra

Sonia (Russian) *see* Sophia

Sophia (Greek) wisdom
Also Beathag, Sadhbh, Sadhbha, Senya, Sifia, Sofia, Sofie, Sonia, Sonja, Sonya, Sophie, Sophy, Zosia, Zsofia

Sorcha (Celtic) *see* Sarah

Stacie *see* Anastasia, Eustacia

Stella (Latin) *see* Esther

Stephanie (French) from the Greek for 'crown or garland'
Feminine form of Stephen
Also Estaphania, Ettienette, Stefanie, Steffanie, Steffie, Stepania, Stephana, Stephania, Stephena, Stevana, Stevania, Stevena, Stevie

Sukie *see* Susan

Susan (Hebrew) lily
Also Sosanna, Su, Sue, Suisan, Suke, Sukey, Sukie, Susana, Susanna, Susannah, Suse, Susette, Susie, Suska, Susy, Suzann, Suzanna, Suzanne, Suze, Suzette, Suzie, Zosa, Zsa Zsa, Zsuzsa, Zusanne

Swanhilda (Old German) swan battle-maiden

Sybil (Greek) prophetess
Also Sevilla, Sibeal, Sibella, Sibelle, Sibil, Sibila, Sibilla, Sibyl, Sibylla, Sibylle, Sybilla, Sybillina, Sybylla

Sydney (Old English) from St
  Denis
  Feminine form of Sidney
  Also Cydney, Sydnee

Sylvia (Latin) one who lives in
  the forest
  Also Ailvia, Silva, Silvana,
  Silvia, Silvie, Silvija, Sylva,
  Sylvana, Zilvia

T

Tabitha (Aramaic) gazelle

Tace (Latin) silence and peace
Also Tacye

Tacita (Latin) silent

Tahira (Arabic) pure

Tamara (Hebrew) a palm tree
Also Tamar, Tammie, Tammy

Tamarind (Arabic) date from
India

Tammy *see* Tamara

Tamsin *see* Thomasina

Tansy (Latin) tenacious, name
for the yellow-flowered herb

Tanya *see* Titania

Tara (Gaelic) crag or tower,
place name of the historic
seat of ancient Irish kings

Tarn (Scandinavian) mountain
lake

Tatiana (Latin) silver-haired
Also Tatianas, Tatianna,
Tatjana

Tatum (Old English) cheerful or
joyful one
Feminine form of Tate

Tavia *see* Octavia

Tegan (Celtic) doe

Tempe (Greek) beautiful,
delightful, charming

Teresa *see* Theresa

Tessa (Greek) *see* Theresa

Thalia (Greek) blooming
Also Talia

Thanh (Chinese) blue

Thea (Greek) goddess
See also Althea, Anthea,
Dorothy (Dorothea),
Theodora

Thecla (Greek) divine
Also Thecle, Thekla

Thelma (Greek) nursling
Also Thelmai

Theodora (Greek) gift of
God
Feminine form of Theodore
Also Fedora, Feodora,
Teodora, Thea, Theodosia
See also Dorothy

Theophila (Greek) loved by
God
Also Theofilia

Theresa (Latin) to harvest
Also Teresa, Terese, Teresija,
Teresina, Teresita, Tereza,
Terry, Tessa, Therese,
Theresia, Tracie, Tracy, Tresa,
Tresca, Tressa

Thetis (Greek) silver-footed

Thomasina (Aramaic) a twin
Feminine form of Thomas
Also Tamasine, Tamsin,
Tamzin, Thomasin,
Thomasine

Thora (Old Norse) the
thunderer
Feminine of Thor

Thyrza (Greek) staff or wand

Tiffany (Greek) when God was
made known
Also Epifania, Epiphanie,
Theophania, Tifaine, Tifanie,
Tiffanie, Tiffeny, Tiphanie

Tina *see* Augusta (Augustina),
Christine, Clementine,
Elizabeth (Bettina), Martina,
Valentina

Ting (Chinese) graceful

Titania (Greek) titaness
Also Tania, Tanya

Toinette *see* Antonia
(Antoinette)

Tomi (Japanese) rich

Toni *see* Antonia

Tonya (Russian) *see* Antonia

Topaz (Greek) jewel name for a
precious yellow stone

Tourmaline (Sri Lankan) jewel

Tracy (Old English) from the
Latin for 'bold, courageous
one'
Also Tracey, Tracie
See also Theresa

Trixie *see* Beatrice

Trudy (Old German) loved one
See also Gertrude

Tsing (Chinese) pure and subtle

Tuesday (Old English) born on
Tuesday
Also Mardi

Tuyet (Chinese) white as snow

U

Ula (Celtic) jewel of the sea

Ultima (Latin) the ultimate or last

Umeko (Japanese) plum blossom

Una (Latin) one
Also Ona, Oona, Oonagh

Undine (Latin) water sprite
Also Ondine, Undene, Undina

Urania (Greek) the sky

Ursula (Latin) she-bear
Also Orsa, Orsola, Sula, Ursa, Ursel, Ursola, Ursule, Ursulette, Ursulina, Ursuline

V

Valda (Old German) a warrior
Also Valina, Velda

Valentina (Latin) valiant and strong one
Feminine form of Valentine
Also Valencia, Valentia, Valida

Valerie (Latin) strong and healthy one
Feminine form of Valerian
Also Valaree, Valeria, Valery, Valoree

Valma (Welsh) a mayflower
Also Valmai

Vanessa (Greek) butterfly
Also Phanessa, Vanesa

Vanka (Russian) *see* Anne

Vanora (Scottish) *see* Genevieve

Vashti (Persian) beautiful
Also Vashta, Vashtee, Vashtia

Velda (Old German) inspired wisdom

Velma *see* Wilhelmina

Velvet (Latin) a fleece

Venetia (Latin) *see* Gwyneth

Venus (Latin) the goddess of love

Vera (Latin) faith, truth
Also Vere, Verena, Verene, Veridiana, Verina, Verine, Verity, Verla
See also Veronica

Veridiana (Spanish) *see* Vera

Verity *see* Vera

Veronica (Latin) of or belonging to an image
Also Veronice, Veronike, Veronique
See also Vera

Victoria (Latin) victorious conquerer
Feminine form of Victor
Also Victoire, Victorija, Victorine, Viktoria, Vitoria, Vittoria
See also Queenie

Vida (Hebrew) *see* Davina

Viola (Latin) *see* Violet

Violet (Old French) flower name
Also Ianthe, Iolanda, Iolanthe, Jolanda, Jolande, Joletta, Viola, Violante, Viole, Violetta, Violette, Yolanda, Yolande, Yolante, Yolanthe, Yolette

Virgilia (Latin) a genus of trees

Virginia (Latin) pure, virgin
  Also Virginie
Vita *see* Davina
Vivien (Latin) vital, alive

Feminine form of Vivian
Also Vivian, Viviana, Vivianne,
Vivienne, Vivyan, Vyvian,
Vyvyan

W

Wanda (Old German) the
wanderer
Also Wandis, Wenda,
Wendelin, Wendeline, Wendy
Wendy *see* Wanda
Wenona (German, Old English)
joy, bliss
Also Wenonah, Winona,
Wynona
Wilhelmina (Old German)
resolute protector
Feminine form of William
(Wilhelm)

Also Guglielma, Guillelmina,
Guillelmine, Guillemette,
Minella, Velma, Vilhelmina,
Vilma, Wilhelma, Wilhelmine,
Willa, Willamina, Willette,
Wilma, Wilmette, Wylma
Willow (English) name of a tree
Winifred (Old German)
peaceful friend
Also Winifrid, Winny
Winsome (English) pleasant or
attractive
Wynne (Celtic) fair

X Y Z

Xanthe (Greek) golden-haired
Xaviera (Arabic) the saviour
Xenia (Greek) hospitable
  Also Xena, Xene, Zenia
Xylia (Greek) of the forest
Yasmine (Arabic) *see* Jasmine
Yedda (Old German) the singer
Yei (Japanese) flourishing
Yen (Chinese) beautiful,
  charming, pretty
Yet-Kwai (Chinese) beautiful as
  a rose
Yetta (Old English) the given
Yoko (Japanese) determined
  woman
Yolande (Old French) *see*
  Violet
Yoshi (Japanese) respectful
Yuri (Japanese) lily

Yvonne (French) the archer
  Feminine form of Yves
  Also Evonne, Ivette, Yevette,
  Yvette
Zada (Arabic) (prosperous
  Also Zadah
Zandra *see* Alexandra
Zane *see* Jane
Zara (Persian) *see* Sarah
Zenda (Persian) womanly
  Also Zendah
Zenobia (Greek) father's
  ornament
  Also Zenobie, Zenovia
Zerlinda (Hebrew) of the dawn
  Also Zerlina
Zoe (Greek) life
  Also Zoia
Zsa Zsa (Hungarian) *see* Susan

BOYS' NAMES

A

Aaron (Hebrew) high mountain
Also Aharoun, Aron, Haroun

Abadi (Arabic) eternal

Abbot (Old English) abbey
father

Abdul (Arabic) servant, son
Also Abdel

Abdullah (Arabic) servant of
Allah

Abel (Hebrew) the breath
Also Abell, Abelot, Able, Hebel

Abner (Hebrew) father of light

Abraham (Hebrew) father of
multitudes
Also Abira, Abrahamo,
Abramo, Arum, Ibrahim

Absalom (Hebrew) father of
peace

Abu (Arabic) father
Also Abou

Ace (Hebrew) unity or the unit,
one who excels

Achilles (Greek) without lips
Also Achille

Adair (Scottish) from the oak-
tree ford

Adam (Hebrew) of the red earth
Also Adamo, Adan, Adao,
Adhamh

Adrian (Latin) of the Adriatic
Also Adriano, Adrien, Arne,
Arrian, Hadrian

Aeneas *see* Angus

Ahmed (Arabic) highly praised

Aidan (Celtic) little fiery one
Also Edan, Egan

Aiken (Old English) the oaken

Ainsley (Old English) Ain's
meadow
Also Ainslee, Ainslie

Airlie *see* Earl

Ajax (Greek) earthy

Akira (Japanese) intelligent

Akiyama (Japanese) autumn

Aladdin (Arabic) servant of
Allah

Alcander (Greek) strong-
minded

Alan (Celtic) handsome,
harmonious one
Also Ailean, Ailin, Alain,
Aland, Alano, Alawn, Allan,
Allen, Allyn, Aluon, Alun,
Alunn, Eilian

Alard (Old German) hard and
noble

Alaric (Old German) to rule all

Alastair (Gaelic) *see* Alexander

Alban (Latin) white; of Alba
Also Alben, Albin
See also Aubin

Albert (Old German) noble and
bright
Also Adalbert, Adelbert,
Adelberto, Adelbrecht, Ailbert,
Albertino, Alberto, Albrecht,
Albret, Aubert, Elbert,
Ethelbert

Aldo (Old German) *see* Aldous

Aldous (Old German) from the
old house
Also Aldis, Aldo, Aldus

Alexander (Greek) protector of
mankind
Also Alasdair, Alastair, Alec,
Aleck, Alejandro, Aleksandras,
Aleksandre, Aleksandus,
Alessandro, Alex, Alexandre,
Alexandros, Alexandru,
Alexio, Alexis, Alick, Alistair,
Alister, Allesandro, Allister,
Alsandair, Alysander, Sasha,
Xan

Alfred (Old German) elf
counsel
Also Alfredo, Alfrid, Alvere,
Auvere, Avery

Algernon (French) with the
whiskers

Ali (Arabic) exalted one

Alistair (Gaelic) *see* Alexander

Allan/Allen *see* Alan

Almeric (Old German) work to
rule
Also Americ, Emeric
See also Eric

Alon (Hebrew) oak tree
Also Allon

Aloysius (French) *see* Lewis

Alphonso (Old German) noble
and ready for battle
Also Affonso, Alfons, Alfonse,
Alonso, Alonzo, Alphonso,
Alphonsus

Alton (Old English) dweller in
the old town

Alvin (Old German) friend of all
or noble friend
Also Aloin, Alvan, Alvino,
Alwin, Alwyn, Elvin

Alvis *see* Elvis

Amadeus (Latin) beloved of
God

Ambrose (Greek) immortal
one
Also Ambrogio, Ambroise,
Ambros, Ambrosi, Ambrosio,
Ambrosius, Ambroz, Ambrozij

Amery (Old French) divine
Also Amory, Emery

Amos (Hebrew) strong,
courageous

Ananda (Sanskrit) a blessing

Anatole (Greek) rising sun
Also Anatol, Anatolio, Anatoly,
Antal

Anders (Scandinavian) *see* Andrew

Andre (French) *see* Andrew

Andrew (Greek) strong or manly
Also Aindreas, Anders, Andre, Andreadis, Andreas, Andrei, Andreiu, Andres, Andrey, Andrzej

Angel (Greek) a heavenly messenger
Also Agnolo, Angelo

Angus (Scottish) unique choice
Also Aeneas, Aonghus

Anthony (Latin) inestimable; beyond price
Also Anntoin, Anthin, Anti, Antoine, Anton, Antonij, Antonin, Antonio, Antonius, Antony, Tonio, Tony

Apollo (Greek) name of the sun god

Aquila (Latin) eagle

Archibald (German) noble and truly bold
Also Achimbald, Archaimbauld, Archambault, Arcibaldo, Gilleasbuig

Arden (Old English) dwelling place

Arian (Greek) of Aries, the god of war
Also Arianus, Arius

Ariel (Hebrew) lion of God

Aristotle (Greek) best of the thinkers

Armand (French) *see* Herman

Armstrong (Old English) strong arm

Arnold (Old German) powerful eagle
Also Arend, Arnaldo, Arnaud, Arne, Arnhold, Arno, Arnoldo, Arnoud, Arnulfo, Arny

Arthur (Celtic) strong as a bear
Also Artair, Artor, Artur, Arturo, Artus

Asa (Hebrew) healer

Asbjorn (Norse) divine bear

Ascott (Old English) eastern cottage

Asher (Hebrew) happy one or laughing one

Ashley (Old English) of the ash tree
Also Ashford, Ashlee

Aston (Old English) eastern place

Atalik (Hungarian) like his father

Athol (Scottish) place name
Also Athole

Aubin (Old French) blond
Also Aubin, Auburn, Aubyn
See also Alban

Aubrey (Old French) king of the fairies
Also Auberon, Oberon

Augustine (Latin) venerated
  Also Agostino, Agoston,
  Auguistin, Austen, Austin
  See also Augustus
Augustus (Latin) the high,
  honoured, mighty
  Also Agosto, August, Auguste,
  Augusto
  See also Augustine

Austin *see* Augustine
Avery (Old English) *see* Alfred
Axel (Old Norse) divine peace
Aylmer (Old English) noble and
  famous
  Also Elmer

B

Baden (German) bath

Bailey (Old French) bailiff
Also Baily

Baldric (Old German) bold
ruler

Baldwin (Old German) bold
protector
Also Baldovino, Baudoin,
Baudouin, Boden, Bowden,
Maldwyn

Banquo (Celtic) white
Also Banan

Baptist (Greek) one who
baptises
Also Baptiste, Battiste

Bard (Irish–Gaelic) poet and
singer

Barnaby (Aramaic) son of
consolation
Also Barna, Barnaba,
Barnabas, Barnabe, Barnabus,
Barnebas, Barney, Bernabe

Barnard *see* Bernard

Barret (Old German) bear
rule
Also Barrett

Barry (Celtic) fine marksman,
spear
Also Barrie

Bartholomew (Hebrew) son of
Talmai, war-like son
Also Bart, Bartek, Bartel,
Bartelemy, Barthel,
Barthelemi, Bartholomaus,
Bartholome, Bartolomeo,
Bartolomeus, Barton,
Parlan

Basil (Greek) kingly, royal
Also Basile, Basileos, Basilio,
Basilius, Bazel, Vasilos,
Vassily

Bastian *see* Sebastian

Baxter (Old English) baker

Beau (French) handsome

Beaumont (Old French) the
beautiful mountain

Beauregard (Old French)
handsome face

Bede (Old German) prayer

Ben (Hebrew) son
Also Benn
See also Benedict, Benjamin,
Benoni

Benedict (Latin) the blessed
and of the benediction
Also Bendix, Benedetto,
Benedick, Benedicto,
Benedictus, Benedikt,

Benedix, Bengt, Benito,
Bennett, Benoit, Benzel

Benjamin (Hebrew) son of my
right hand
Also Bannerjee, Beathan,
Beniamino
See also Benson

Bennett (English) *see* Benedict

Benson (Hebrew–English) son
of Benjamin

Benvenuto (Italian) the right way

Berenger (Old German) a bear,
spear

Bernard (Old German) as brave
as a bear
Also Barnard, Barnett,
Bearnard, Bernardo, Bernat,
Berngard, Bernhard, Bernhart,
Burnard

Berthold (Old German) bright
ruler
Also Berthoud, Bertolde,
Bertoldi, Bertolt, Bertuccio

Bertram (Old German) bright
raven
Also Bartok, Bartram, Beltran,
Bertrand, Bertrando

Bevan (Celtic) a young archer
Also Beavan, Beaven, Beven,
Bevin

Bjorn (Scandinavian) bear

Blaine (Old English) to bubble
or blow
Also Blain, Blane, Blayne

Blair (Celtic) a place, a suitable
battlefield

Blaise (Latin) stammerer
Also Biagio, Blas, Blase,
Blasien, Blasio, Blasius,
Blayse, Blaze

Blake (Old English) dark or black

Bland (Latin) mild and gentle

Bob *see* Robert

Bonar (Old French) courteous

Boris (Russian) a fighter

Bowen (Celtic) son of Owen

Boyce (French) of the woods

Boyd (Celtic) fair-haired

Braden (Old English) from the
broad valley

Bradford (Old English) from
the broad river crossing

Bradley (Old English) from the
broad meadow
Also Brad, Bradlee

Brand (Old English) firebrand

Brandon (Celtic) raven
Also Brandan, Branwell

Bray (Old English) brow of the
hill

Brecon (Welsh) after the
mountains in Wales, the
Brecon Beacons

Breese (Old English) son of
Rhees

Brendan (Celtic) dweller by the
beacon
Also Bredon

Brenton (Old English) the steep or the tall and erect
Also Brent

Brett (Celtic) from Brittany or a Breton

Brewster (Old German) a brewer

Brian (Celtic) strength
Also Branko, Briano, Briant, Brien, Brion, Bryan, Bryant, Bryon

Brice (Celtic) swift or ambitious
Also Bricot, Brisson, Bryce, Bryson

Brinsley (Old English) Brin's meadow
Also Brinsleigh

Brock (Old English) a badger

Broderick (Middle English) from the broad ridge

Brodie (Irish) a ditch
Also Brody

Bruce (Old French) of the brush or of the thicket

Bruno (German) brown

Burleigh (Old English) fort in a clearing
Also Burl, Burley, Burly
See also Burton

Burton (Old English) dweller at the fortified town

Bryan *see* Brian

Bryce *see* Brice

Byron (Middle English) from the cottage or cowman

C

Cadman (Celtic) warrior
Cadmus (Greek) to the east
Caesar (Latin) long head of
hair
Also Casar, Caesario,
Caesarius, Cesar, Cesare
Caffar (Celtic) helmet
Cain (Hebrew) possessed
Also Caine
Caleb (Hebrew) bold and
impetuous
Callaghan (Irish) strike
Also Callahan
Callum (Gaelic) *see* Columba
Calvin (Latin) the bald
Cameron (Gaelic) crooked
nose
Camillus (Etruscan) attendant
at religious ceremonies
Also Camille, Camillo
Campbell (Gaelic) curved
mouth
Carl (German) *see* Charles
Carlos (Spanish) *see* Charles
Carrick (Irish) rocky headland
Carroll (Celtic) champion
fighter or warrior
Carter (Old English) maker or
driver of carts

Cary (Celtic) one who lives in a
castle
Also Carey
See also Charles
Casey (Irish) brave
Casimir (Polish) proclamation
of peace
Also Kasimir
Caspar *see* Gaspar
Cassidy (Irish) clever
Cassius (Latin) vain
Cecil (Latin) blind
Also Cecile, Ceilius
Cedric (Old English) bounteous
and friendly
Ceri *see* Kerry
Chad (Old English) warrior
Chaim (Hebrew) life
Also Hyram
Chandler (Old French) candle
maker
Chandra (Sanskrit) moon
Charles (Old German) virile
and strong man
Also Carey, Carl, Carlo, Carlos,
Carolus, Cary, Karel, Karl,
Karoly, Tearlach
Charlton (Old English) of
Charles' or the man's farm

Also Carleton, Carlton

Chauncey (French) chancellor, church official

Cheng (Chinese) accomplish, succeed

Chester (Latin) of the fortified camp

Chilton (Old English) of the children's farm

Christian (Latin) a Christian
Also Chrestien, Chretien, Christen, Christiano, Christien, Karstin, Krispin, Kristian, Kruschan

Christopher (Greek) bearer of Christ
Also Christof, Christofer, Christoforo, Christoph, Christophe, Christophorus, Christoval, Cristobal, Crysteffor, Gillecriosd, Kristof, Kristofor, Kristopas, Kristopher, Kristova

Chun (Chinese) spring

Clarence (Latin) illustrious or bright
Also Clancy

Clark (Old English) a learned man or cleric

Claude (Latin) the lame
Also Claud, Claudio, Claudius, Klaud

Claus *see* Nicholas

Clayton (Old English) dweller in the clay town
Also Clay

Clement (Latin) merciful
Also Clemens, Clemente, Clementius, Clemento, Keleman, Klemens

Clifford (Old English) of the cliff ford
Also Cliff

Clinton (Old English) hilltop town
Also Clint

Clive (English) cliff

Clunies (Gaelic) resting place

Cohen (Hebrew) priest

Colby (Old English) of Cole's farm

Cole (Celtic) pledge

Colin *see* Columba

Columba (Latin) dove
Also Cailean, Callum, Colan, Colin, Collin, Colum
See also Malcolm

Conan (Celtic) high and mighty
Also Conal, Connell, Konan, Kynan

Connor (Irish) lofty aims or high desire
Also Conor

Conrad (Old German) wise or bold adviser

Also Conrade, Conrado, Cort,
Koenraad, Konrad, Konradin,
Kort, Kurt

Conroy (Irish) wise man

Constantine (Latin) firm in
faith
Also Constantin, Constantino,
Constantinos, Kastaden,
Konstantin, Kostodon

Corbin (Old French) raven

Cormac (Greek) tree trunk
Also Cormack, Cormick

Cornelius (Latin) a horn
Also Corneille, Cornelio,
Cornelis, Kornelius

Cosmo (Greek) order and
harmony
Also Cosimo, Cosme

Courtney (Old French) dweller
at court

Craig (Celtic) from the stony
hill or crag

Crichton (Gaelic) boundary
Also Creighton

Crispin (Latin) curly haired
Also Crispianus, Crispino,
Crispo, Crispus, Krispijn,
Krispin

Curtis (Old French) courteous
Also Curt, Kurt

Cuthbert (Old English) famous,
bright

Cyrano (Greek) of Cyrene

Cyriack (Greek) lordly
Also Syriack

Cyril (Greek) lord and
master
Also Cirillo, Cirilo, Cyrill,
Cyrille, Cyrillus

Cyrus (Greek) throne

D

Dale (Old English) from the dale or valley

Damian *see* Damon

Damon (Greek) the tamed or taming
Also Damian, Damiano, Damiao, Damien, Damir

Dane (English) from Denmark
Also Dana

Daniel (Hebrew) God is my judge
Also Danelo, Danilo, Dannel, Taniel

Dante (Italian) long-lasting
Also Duran, Durand

Darcy (Old French) from the ark or stronghold
Also D'Arcy

Darius (Persian) possessing wealth
Also Darian, Darien

Darrell (Old English) darling or beloved one
Also Darrel, Daryl, Derrell

Darren (Gaelic) little one
Also Daran, Darrin, Dorian

David (Hebrew) beloved; loved by God
Also Dafod, Daibidh, Davidas, Davidde, Davide, Davis,
Dawfydd, Dawud, Devi, Dewi, Taffy, Tavid

Davis *see* David

Dean (Old English) from the valley
Also Deane, Dene

Decimus (Latin) tenth child

Declan (Irish) unknown origin; after St Declan

Delano (French) of the night

Demetrios (Greek) sacred
Also Demetri, Dimitry

Dennis (Greek) follower of the god of wine, Dionysos
Also Denis, Denys, Dion, Dionigio, Dionisio, Dionysius, Dionysos

Denzil (Cornish) high
Also Denzell

Deodatus (Latin) given by or to God
Also Deodonatus

Derek (German) ruler of the people
Also Derk, Derrick, Deryk, Diederich, Dirck, Dirk

Dermot (Celtic) a free man
Also Dermott, Diarmaid, Diarmid, Diarmit, Duibhne

Derwin (Old English) beloved
friend
Also Derryn, Derwyn

Desmond (Irish) man of South
Munster

Dexter (Latin) right-handed or
skilful man

Dillon (Gaelic) faithful one
Also Dylan

Dirk *see* Derek

Dobroslav (Slavonic) glorious

Dominic (Latin) belonging to
the Lord
Also Domingo, Dominichino,
Dominick, Dominik,
Dominique, Domnech

Donald (Gaelic) prince of
the universe; ruler of the
world
Also Donal, Donley, Donnal,
Donnell, Tauno

Donatien (French) given
Also Donat, Donatus, Donnet

Donovan (Irish) dark brown

Dorian *see* Darren

Dougal *see* Dugald

Douglas (Celtic) from the dark
blue water
Also Douglass

Doyle (Irish) dark foreigner

Dudley (Old English) from the
lea or meadow

Dugald (Irish) dark stranger
Also Dougal

Duncan (Celtic) brown warrior

Durand (French) *see* Dante

Dwayne (Gaelic) little dark one
Also Duane

Dwight (English) white or blond
one

Dylan (Welsh) man of the sea
Also Dillon

E

Eamon (Irish) *see* Edmund

Earl (Old English) nobleman or chief
Also Airlie, Earle, Erle, Errol

Ebenezer (Hebrew) stone of help

Edgar (Old English) bright or lucky spear
Also Eadgar, Edgard, Edgardo

Edmund (Old English) prosperous protector
Also Eadmund, Eamon, Edmond, Edmondo, Emmon

Edsel (Old English) rich hall

Edward (Old English) prosperous friend or guardian
Also Duarte, Edouard, Eduard, Eduardo, Eduart, Edvard, Edwardo, Edwardus

Edwin (Old English) rich or happy friend
Also Eduino, Edwyn

Egan *see* Aidan

Egbert (Old English) bright sword

Egor (Russian) *see* George

Eldred (Old English) old counsel
Also Aldred

Eleazar (Hebrew) the Lord is helper

Eli *see* Elias

Elias (Hebrew) Jehovah is God
Also Eli, Elia, Elijah, Elijas, Elisha, Elliot, Elliott, Ellis, Ely

Ellery (English) sweetly spoken

Elliot (English) *see* Elias

Ellis (English) *see* Elias

Elmer *see* Aylmer

Elroy (Old French) the king

Elton (Old English) of the old town
Also Alton

Elvis (Old Norse) all wise
Also Alvis

Emery (Old German) to work and rule
Also Amerigo, Amery, Emeri, Emeric, Emerson, Emmery, Emory

Emil (Old German) industrious
Also Emile, Emilio

Emmanuel (Hebrew) God is with us
Also Emanuel, Emanuele, Immanuel
See also Manuel

Emmett (Old English) meeting
streams
Also Emmet, Emmit, Emmott
Enrico (Italian) *see* Henry
Enzio (Italian) *see* Henry
Ephraim (Hebrew) doubly
fruitful
Also Ephram, Ephrem
Erasmus (Greek) desired or
friendly
Ercole (Italian) *see* Hercules
Erhard (Old German) strong
and resolved
Eric (Old Norse) powerful
ruler
Also Eirik, Erich, Erick, Erih,
Erik, Errki
Ernest (Old German) earnest
Also Eernest, Ernesto,
Ernestus, Ernst, Hernais
Errol *see* Earl
Erwin *see* Irving
Esau (Hebrew) hairy
Esmond (Old English) grace,
beauty
Ethan (Hebrew) steadfast,
strong
Ethelbert *see* Albert

Etienne (French) *see* Stephen
Euan *see* Evan
Eubule (Greek) he of good
counsel
Eudo (Old Norse) child
Eugene (Greek) nobility,
excellence
Also Eugen, Eugenij, Eugenio,
Eugenius, Yevgenij
Eustace (Greek) fruitful
Also Eustachas, Eustache,
Eustachio, Eustaquio, Eustas
Evan (Welsh) the young
Also Euan, Ewan, Ewen, Jevon,
Owen
See also John
Everard (Old English) strong or
brave as a boar
Also Eberhard, Eberhart,
Everado, Evered, Everett,
Everhart, Evraud
Ewen *see* Evan
Ezekiel (Hebrew) strength of
God
Also Ezechiel, Ezechiele,
Ezequiel
Ezra (Hebrew) helper
Also Esdras, Esra

F

Fabian (Latin) ancient Roman family name derived from bean grower
Also Fabien, Fabio, Fabius, Fafiano

Fabrice (French) mechanic
Also Fabrician, Fabricius

Fagan (Gaelic) fiery one
Also Fagin

Faramond (Old German) journey, protection

Farley (Old English) clearing with ferns
Also Farleigh

Farouk (Arabic) to know right from wrong

Farquhar (Gaelic) manly, brave

Faustas (Latin) fortunate, lucky
Also Faust, Faustus

Felix (Latin) happy
Also Felice, Feliks, Phelim

Ferdinand (Old German) adventurer
Also Ferdinando, Fernando, Ferrand, Ferrante, Hernando

Fergus (Celtic) the best choice
Also Fearghas, Feargus

Ferris (Irish) *see* Peter

Fidel (Latin) faithful
Also Fidele, Fidelio, Fildes, Filelio

Findlay (Celtic) fair hero
Also Finlay, Finn

Finian (Celtic) fair child

Flannan (Celtic) blood-red

Fletcher (Old French) arrow-maker and seller

Florian (Latin) flourishing

Floyd *see* Lloyd

Flynn (Irish) son of the red-haired one

Forbes (Scottish) man of prosperity, owner of many fields

Francis (Latin) free; a Frenchman
Also Ferenc, Francesco, Franchot, Francisco, Franciskus, Franciszek, Franco, Francois, Frane, Frank, Frans, Frants, Franz, Franzisk

Frank *see* Francis

Franklin (Middle English) not in bondage, freeholder
Also Francklin, Franklyn

Fraser (Old English) curly-haired
Also Frazer
Frederick (Old German) peaceful ruler
Also Farruco, Frederic, Frederico, Fredericus, Frederigo, Frederik, Frederikos, Fredric, Fredrik, Freerik, Fridrich, Friedrich, Fritz
Fu (Chinese) man
Fu-Hai (Chinese) man of the lake

G

Gabor (Hungarian) *see* Gabriel

Gabriel (Hebrew) messenger of
God
Also Gabel, Gabela, Gabor,
Gabriele, Gabriello, Gavril

Gamel (Old Norse) old

Gandolfo (German) progress of
the wolf

Garcia (Spanish) *see* Gerald

Gareth (Welsh) gentle
See also Gary

Garfield (Old English) field of
war
See also Gary

Garnet (Middle English) dark
red stone

Garth (Old Norse) from the
garden, a yardkeeper

Gary *diminutive* of Gareth,
Garfield and Gerald
Also Garey, Gari, Garrie

Gaspar (Persian) treasure
master
Also Caspar, Casper, Gaspard,
Gaspardo, Gasparo, Gasper,
Jasper, Kaspar, Kaspe,
Kasper

Gaspard (French) *see* Gaspar

Gaston (French) from Gascony

Gavin (Welsh) white hawk
Also Gauvain, Gavan, Gaven,
Gawain, Gawayne, Gawen,
Gawin

Gene *see* Eugene

Geoffrey (Old German) divine
peace
Also Geoff, Geoffroi, Giofredo,
Godfrey, Godofredo, Gofredo,
Gotfryd, Jeffery, Jeffrey, Jeffroi

George (Greek) tiller of the soil
Also Djuro, Egor, Georas,
Georg, Georges, Georgius,
Giorgio, Gyorgy, Igor, Jerzy,
Jiri, Jorge, Seiorse, Yorick,
Yrjo, Yuri

Gerald (Old German) spear and
rule
Also Garcia, Gearalt, Geralde,
Geraud, Gerold, Gerrit, Gerry,
Gieraud, Giraldo

Gerard (Old German) spear and
hard
Also Garrett, Gebhard,
Gerardo, Geraud, Gerhard,
Gerhart, Gerry, Gherardino

Gerry *see* Gerald and Gerard

Gervaise (French) *see* Jarvis

Giannino (Italian) *see* John

Gideon (Hebrew) feller or hewer

Gifford (Old German) bold gift

Gil (Hebrew) joy
See also Gilbert, Giles

Gilbert (Old German) bright pledge
Also Gilbertas, Gilberto, Gilibeirt, Gilleabart, Giselbert, Guilbert

Gilchrist (Gaelic) servant of Christ

Giles (Greek) youthful; wearer of the goatskin
Also Egide, Egidio, Egidius, Gil, Gilles, Gillie

Giorgio (Italian) *see* George

Giovanni (Italian) *see* John

Glen (Celtic) of the glen or valley
Also Glenn, Glyn, Glynn, Glynne

Goddard (Old German) God and hard

Godfrey *see* Geoffrey

Godwin (Old English) God's friend

Goldwin (Old English) golden friend

Gonzales (Spanish) wolf of war
Also Gonzalo

Gordon (Gaelic) from the cornered hill
Also Gordan, Gorden

Gough (Welsh) red-haired

Graeme *see* Graham

Graham (Old English) from the grey home
Also Graeme, Grahame, Grame

Grant (Old French) the great or tall one

Grantham (Old English) the big meadow
Also Grantland, Grantley

Granville (Old French) from the great estate or town

Gregory (Greek) vigilant or watchful
Also Greagoir, Greg, Gregg, Gregoire, Gregor, Gregorie, Gregorio, Gregorius, Gregos, Greig, Grigg, Grigor, Grigori, Grigorij, Grigory, Griogair, Grioghar

Griffith (Welsh) strong lord

Guilhermo (Spanish) *see* William

Guiseppe (Italian) *see* Joseph

Gunther (German) battle army
Also Gunthar

Gustavus (Old German) staff of God
Also Gustav

Guy (Old German) perhaps meaning wood or a guide
Also Guido

Gwyn (Welsh) blessed

H

Habib (Arabic) the beloved

Hacon (Old Norse) useful, handy
  Also Haakon

Hadden (Old English) from the heather of the moors
  Also Haden

Hadrian *see* Adrian

Hagan (Gaelic) the young one

Hai (Chinese) of the sea or lake

Hamilton (Scottish) crooked hill

Hamish (Gaelic) *see* Jacob (James)

Hamon (Old German) house or home

Hannibal (Phoenician) by the grace of Baal

Hans (German) *see* John

Hardy (Old German) robust and enduring

Harold (Old English) ruler of the army
  Also Aralt, Harailt, Harald, Haroldas, Harris, Harry, Herold

Harry *see* Harold and Henry

Harvey (Breton) battle-worthy
  Also Hervey

Hayden (Old English) from the hedge or valley
  Also Haydon, Haydn

Heath (Old English) from the heath or heather

Heathcliff (Old English) cliff and heather

Heathcote (Old English) cottage among the heath

Hector (Greek) steadfast
  Also Ettore

Heinrich (German) *see* Henry

Helmut (German) courage and fame

Henry (Old German) home ruler
  Also Eanruig, Enrico, Enrikas, Enrique, Enzio, Hamlyn, Hanraoi, Harry, Heikki, Heine, Heinrich, Heinz, Hendrick, Hendrik, Henk, Henri, Henrici, Henricus, Henrik, Henriot, Henrique

Herbert (Old German) brilliant warrior
  Also Eberto, Harbert, Hebert, Herbertas, Heriberto, Hoireabard

Hercules (Greek) lordly fame
  Also Ercole, Heracles, Hercule

Herman (Old German) warrior
Also Armand, Armando, Armant, Armin, Ermanno, Ermin, Harman, Harmann, Harmon, Hermando, Hermon
Hermes (Greek) noble
Hilary (Latin) cheerful and merry
Also Hilaire, Hilario, Hillary, Hillery, Ilario
Hiram (Hebrew) God is high
Hoa (Vietnamese) peace-loving
Homer (Greek) pledge, security
Also Homere, Homerus, Omero
Horace (Latin) keeper of the hours of light
Also Horacio, Horatio, Horatius, Horats, Orazio

Howard (Old English) brave in heart and mind
Hu (Chinese) a tiger, brave
Hubert (Old German) bright heart and mind
Also Hoibeard, Huberto, Hugibert, Ulberto
Hugh (Old German) thoughtful mind
Also Aodh, Aoidh, Hu, Hugo, Hugues, Ugo
Hugo (German) *see* Hugh
Humphrey (Old German) protector of peace
Also Humfrey, Humfrid, Humfried, Humfry, Hunfredo, Onfroi, Onofre, Onofredo
Hwang Fu (Chinese) rich future
Hyram *see* Chaim

I

Ian (Scottish) *see* John
Ignatius (Latin) ardent; fiery
  Also Ignace, Ignacio, Ignatus,
  Ignaz, Ignazio, Inigo
Igor (Russian) *see* George
Immanuel *see* Emmanuel
Ingemar (Old Norse) famous
  son
  Also Ingmar
Ira (Hebrew) a watcher
Irving (Old English) friend of
  the sea
  Also Erwin, Irvin, Irvine, Irwin

Isaac (Hebrew) laughter
  Also Isaak, Isacco, Izaak
Isaiah (Hebrew) God is helper
Isas (Japanese) meritorious
Israel (Hebrew) ruling with the
  Lord
Ivan (Russian) *see* John
Ives *see* Yves
Ivo *see* Yves
Ivor (Norse) archer
  Also Ifor, Ivar, Iver

J

Jabez (Hebrew) height

Jack *see* John

Jackson (Old English) son of Jack

Jacob (Hebrew) supplanter
Also Diego, Giacobbe, Giacobo, Giacomo, Giacopo, Hamish, Iachimo, Iacovo, Iago, Jacabo, Jaco, Jacobus, Jacques, Jaime, Jakab, Jake, Jakob, Jakov, James, Jan, Jascha, Jayme, Jens, Seamus, Shamus

Jacques (French) *see* Jacob

James *see* Jacob

Jan *see* Jacob, John

Janos (Hungarian) *see* John

Jared (Hebrew) to descend
Also Jaret, Jareth, Jarrath, Jarrod

Jarvis (Old German) sharp spear
Also Gervaise, Jervis

Jason (Greek) healer

Jasper *see* Gaspar

Jean (French) *see* John

Jedidiah (Hebrew) God's friend
Also Jed

Jeffrey *see* Geoffrey

Jeremy (Hebrew) exalted by the Lord
Also Diarmaidh, Geremia, Jeremiah, Jeremias

Jerome (Greek) the holy name
Also Gerome, Geronimo, Jeronimus, Jerrome

Jesse (Hebrew) God's grace; he beholds

Jethro (Hebrew) abundance or excellence

Jevon (Welsh) *see* Evan

Jiang (Chinese) river

Jivanta (Sanskrit) long-lived

Joachim (Hebrew) God will establish
Also Joaquin

Jocelyn *see* Justin

Joel (Hebrew) the Lord is God

Johann (German) *see* John

John (Hebrew) God is gracious
Also Eoghan, Eoin, Evan, Gian, Gianninno, Giovanni, Hannu, Hans, Iaian, Iain, Ian, Iannis, Ioan, Ivan, Jack, Jan, Janos, Jean, Joao, Jock, Johann, Johannes, Jon, Jones, Jonn, Jovica, Juan, Jussi, Seain,

Sean, Seann, Shane, Shawn,
Yiannis, Zane

Jolyon variant of Julius;
popularised in John
Galsworthy's *The Forsyte
Saga*

Jonas (Hebrew) the dove
Also Jonah

Jonathan (Hebrew) gift of the
Lord
Also Jonathon, Jonothon

Jordan (Hebrew) to descend
Also Gioidana, Jordanes,
Jourdain

Joseph (Hebrew) increaser
Also Guiseppe, Josep, Josip,
Jossif, Jozef, Seosaidh, Yusuf

Joshua (Hebrew) God saves

Josiah (Hebrew) healed by the
Lord
Also Josias

Juan *see* John

Jude (Hebrew) praise

Jules (French) *see* Julius

Julian *see* Julius

Julius (Latin) youthful one
Also Giulio, Jules, Julian,
Juliao, Julien, Julio, Julion,
Julot

Justin (Latin) the just
Also Guistino, Iestin, Jocelin,
Jocelyn, Joslyn, Justino,
Justis, Justus, Justyn

K

Kafir (Arabic) infidel

Kai (Persian) king

Kane (Celtic) radiant;
  bright
  Also Caine, Kayne

Karim (Arabic) generous, noble;
  one of the names for god in
  the Koran

Karl (German) *see* Charles

Kaspar *see* Gaspar

Keegan (Irish) little high-
  spirited one

Keenan (Irish) little ancient
  one
  Also Kienan, Kynan

Kieron *see* Kieren

Keith (Gaelic) wood

Kelly (Irish) warrior
  Also Kelley

Kelsey (Old Norse) from the
  water

Kelvin (Old English) sailor's
  friend
  Also Kelvan, Kelven

Kelwin (Celtic) dweller by the
  water

Kendall (Celtic) chief of the
  valley
  Also Kendal

Kenelm (Old English) brave
  helmet
  Also Cenhelm

Kenneth (Gaelic) handsome
  one
  Also Cennydd

Kenrick (Old English) royal
  ruler

Kent (Welsh) bright one

Kenward (Old English) brave
  guard

Kerry (Irish) dark one
  Also Ceri

Kevin (Irish) handsome or kind
  Also Kevan, Keven

Kieren (Irish) small and dark
  Also Cairan, Kieran, Kieron,
  Kyran, Piran

Kilian (Gaelic) small and
  warlike
  Also Kilmer

Kim *see* Kimberley

Kimball (Greek) hollow vessel
  Also Kim

Kimberley (Old English) one
  who rules
  Also Kim

Kingsley (Old English) of the
  king's meadow

Kipp (English) pointed hill, peak

Kirk (Old Norse) a place by the church

Kit *see* Christian and Christopher

Konrad *see* Conrad

Krishna (Sanskrit) black

Krispin *see* Christian and Crispin

Kurt (German) *see* Conrad and Curtis

Kyle (Gaelic) fair and handsome

L

Lachlan (Scottish) warlike
Also Laughlan

Ladislav (Slavonic) glory, power
Also Ladislaus, Laszlo,
Laszolo

Lambert (Old German) bright
land
Also Lambard, Lamberto

Lamont (Old Norse) law man
Also Lamond

Lance (Old German) land
Also Lancelin, Lancelot,
Lanzo, Launcelot

Lancelot (French) *see* Lance

Lang (Old German) the long or
the tall

Larry *see* Laurence

Lars (Scandinavian) *see*
Laurence

Laszlo (Hungarian) *see* Ladislav

Lateef (Arabic) gentle and
pleasant

Latimer (Old French) teacher of
Latin

Laurence (Latin) crowned with
laurel
Also Labhras, Labhruinn,
Larrance, Lars, Laurans,
Lauren, Láurens, Laurent,
Laurenz, Laurie, Lauritz,
Lawrance, Lawrence, Loren,
Lorenz, Lorenzo, Lourenco

Lazarus (Hebrew) one whom
God helps
Also Lazare, Lazaro, Lazzaro,
Lazzo

Lee (Old English) a meadow or
clearing
Also Leigh

Leif (Scandinavian) love
Also Leiv, Lief

Leigh *see* Lee

Leith (Celtic) wide

Leo (Latin) the lion
Also Leon, Levin, Lionel,
Lionello, Lyle, Lyonell

Leonard (Old German) as
strong as a lion
Also Leanardas, Lennard,
Leonardo, Leonerd, Leonhard,
Leonid, Lionardo

Leopold (Old German) bold
people
Also Leopoldo, Leupold,
Luitpold

Leroy (Old French) a king

Leslie (Scottish) from the grey
stronghold

Lester (Old English) from
  Leicester
  Also Leicester
Levi (Hebrew) pledge, united
Lewis (Old German) to hear
  and fight
  Also Alois, Aloys, Aloysius,
  Clovis, Lajos, Lodewijk,
  Lodovico, Louis, Ludovic,
  Ludovicus, Ludvig, Ludwig,
  Lugaidh, Luigi, Luis, Luiz,
  Luthais
Liam (Irish) *see* William
Lincoln (Celtic) from the
  colony by the pool
Lindsay (Old English) of the
  linden tree
  Also Linden, Lindley, Lindon,
  Lindsey, Linsay, Linsey,
  Lyndon

Linus (Greek) flax-coloured hair
Lionel (Old French) *see* Leo
Llewellyn (Old Welsh) lion-like
  leader
  Also Leoline, Llewllyn
Lloyd (Welsh) the grey
  Also Floyd
Lok (Chinese) happiness
Louis (Old French) *see* Lewis
Loy (Chinese) open
Lucian *see* Luke
Ludovic *see* Lewis
Luke (Latin) light
  Also Loukas, Luc, Luca,
  Lucais, Lucas, Lucian,
  Luciano, Lucien, Lucio,
  Lucius, Lukas, Lukaz,
  Luzio
Lyle *see* Leo
Lyndon *see* Lindsay

M

Magnus (Latin) the great
Also Manus

Malachi (Hebrew) messenger of God
Also Malachy

Malcolm (Gaelic) servant of St Columba

Malik (Arabic) master

Malise (Gaelic) servant of Jesus

Malory (Old French) luckless
Also Mallory

Manfred (German) peaceful man

Manning (Old English) son of a good man

Manuel (Spanish) God with us
Also Manovello
See also Emmanuel

Marcel (French) *see* Mark

Mario (Italian) *see* Mark

Mark (Latin) after Mars, the god of war
Also Marc, Marcel, Marcello, Marcellus, Marcelo, Marco, Marcos, Marcus, Mario, Marius, Marko, Markos, Markus
See also Martin

Marmaduke (Celtic) servant of Madoc

Marshall (Old French) the steward

Martin (Latin) after Mars, the god of war
Also Martainn, Marten, Marti, Martijn, Martino, Marton, Martynas
See also Mark

Marvin (Old English) sea friend
Also Mervin, Mervyn, Merwin, Merwyn

Matthew (Hebrew) gift of the Lord
Also Mata, Mateo, Mateusz, Mathaeus, Mathew, Mathhaus, Mathias, Mathieu, Matteo, Mattheus, Matthias, Mattias, Matyas, Mayhew

Maurice (Latin) a Moor
Also Maolmuire, Mauricio, Mauritius, Maurits, Maurizio, Moritz, Morrell, Morris

Maximilian (Latin) the greatest
Also Maksimilian, Massimiliano, Maxim, Maximilanus, Maximiliano, Maximilien, Maximo

Maxwell (Old English) a large well

Maynard (Old German) strength and hardy

Melbourne (Old English) from the mill stream

Melvin (Irish) smooth brow
Also Malvin, Melvyn

Mervin *see* Marvin

Michael (Hebrew) 'who is like God?'
Also Micah, Michan, Micheil, Michel, Michele, Miguel, Mihael, Mihaly, Mikael, Mikhail, Mirko, Mischa, Mitchell

Milan (Latin) the lovable

Miles (Old German) merciful
Also Milo, Myles

Milton (Old English) from the mill town

Ming (Chinese) bright, brilliant

Mitchell *see* Michael

Montague (Old French) from the pointed hill

Montgomery (Old French) from the wealthy one's hill
Also Monty

Morgan (Celtic) from the sea

Morris (English) *see* Maurice

Moses (Egyptian) child
Also Moesen, Moise, Moises, Moshe, Moyse, Mozes

Murdoch (Gaelic) sea man

Murray (Celtic) man of the sea

Myles *see* Miles

Myron (Greek) fragrant ointment

N

Nahum (Hebrew) comforter
Napoleon (Italian) of Naples
Nathan (Hebrew) gift
Nathaniel (Hebrew) gift of
  God
  Also Natanael, Nataniel,
  Nathanael
Ned *see* Edward
Neil (Irish) champion
  Also Neal, Neale, Neall, Neel,
  Neill, Nels, Nial, Niall, Niel,
  Niels, Nigel, Niles, Nils
Nelson (English) son of the
  champion
  Also Nealson, Nilson
Neville (French) new town
  Also Nevil, Nevile
Nicholas (Greek) the people's
  victory
  Also Claus, Miklos, Neacail,

Niccolo, Nickel, Nickolaus,
Nicodemus, Nicol, Nicolaas,
Nicolas, Nicolo, Nikolai,
Nikolay
Nicodemus (Greek) *see*
  Nicholas
Nigel *see* Neil
Nils (Scandinavian) *see* Neil
Ninian (Scottish) the name of a
  saint
  See also Vivian
Noah (Hebrew) rest or comfort
  Also Noach, Noak
Noel (Old French) Christmas
  Also Natal, Natale, Newell,
  Nowell
Nolan (Irish) noble
  Also Noland
Norman (Old English) northern
  man

O

Obadiah (Hebrew) servant of Jehovah

Oberon *see* Aubrey

Octavius (Latin) the eighth child
Also Octavio, Ottavio

Olaf (Old Norse) ancestral relic
Also Aulay, Olaff, Olav

Oliver (Old French) the olive tree, symbol of peace
Also Oliverio, Olivero, Olivier

Omar (Arabic) highest, or first son

Orlando (Italian) *see* Roland

Orville (Old French) from a golden place

Oscar (Old English) God's spear
Also Osgar, Oskar

Osmond (Old English) God's protection

Oswald (Old English) God's power

Othello (Italian) *see* Otto

Otis (Greek) keen of hearing
Also Otys

Otto (Old German) rich
Also Oddo, Odo, Othello, Otho

Owen (Welsh) well-born
Also Owain, Owayne, Ywain
See also Evan

P

Pablo (Spanish) *see* Paul
Paget (French) young attendant
  Also Padget, Page, Pagett,
  Paige
Paolo (Italian) *see* Paul
Pascoe (Middle English) born at
  Easter
  Also Pascal, Pascall, Paschal,
  Pasquale
Patrick (Latin) nobleman
  Also Padraic, Padraig, Padric,
  Padrick, Padruig, Patric,
  Patrice, Patricio, Patrizius,
  Patten
Paul (Latin) small
  Also Paavali, Paavo, Pablo,
  Paolo, Paulin, Paulo, Paulot,
  Pavel, Pavlos, Poul
Pedro (Spanish) *see* Peter
Percival (French) to cut
  through the valley
  Also Parsifal, Percy, Perseval,
  Persifal
Peregrine (Latin) wanderer
  Also Perry
Perry *see* Peregrine, Peter

Perseus (Greek) destroyer
Peter (Greek) stone or rock
  Also Farus, Feoris, Ferris,
  Peadair, Peadar, Peder, pedro,
  Peer, Pekka, Per, Pero, Perren,
  Perrin, Perry, Pete, Petr,
  Petros, Petru, Petrus, Pierce,
  Piero, Pierre, Piers, Piet,
  Pieter, Pietro, Piotr, Pyotr
Phelan (Celtic) a wolf
Phelim (Irish) the ever good
Philip (Greek) lover of horses
  Also Felep, Felope, Filib, Filip,
  Filippo, Phelp, Philipp,
  Philippe, Phillip, Philp, Pileb
Phineas (Hebrew) oracle
Phoenix (Greek) purple;
  mythological bird
Pierce *see* Peter
Piers (French) *see* Peter
Piran (Irish) *see* Kieren
Prentice (Old French) an
  apprentice
  Also Prentiss
Preston (Old English) priest's
  place

Q

Quentin (Latin) the fifth child
Also Quinn, Quinton
Quillon (Latin) sword hilt
Also Quillian

Quincy (French) place name
Quong (Chinese) bright

R

Radcliffe (Old English) red cliff

Radford (Old English) red ford

Raleigh (Old English) red clearing
Also Rawley

Ralph (Old Norse) counsel and wolf
Also Rafe, Raff, Ral, Ralf, Raoul, Rolf, Rolfe, Rolph

Ramsey (Old German) the strong
Also Ramsay

Randal *see* Randolph

Randolph (Old English) wolf's shield
Also Randal, Randall, Randell, Randolf, Randolphus

Raoul (French) *see* Ralph

Raphael (Hebrew) healing by God
Also Rafael, Rafaelle, Rafaello

Raymond (Old German) wise and mighty protector
Also Raimondo, Raimous, Raimund, Raimundo, Ramon, Ray, Reamonn, Redmond, Reymond

Raynor (Old German) mighty army
Also Rainer, Rainier, Rayner

Reece (Old Welsh) ardent one
Also Rees, Reese, Rhett, Rhys, Rice

Reginald (Old English) mighty, powerful and forceful
Also Raghnall, Ranald, Regnaud, Regnault, Reinald, Reinaldo, Reinaldos, Reinhold, Reinold, Reinwald, Renaldos, Renato, Renault, Reynold, Reynolds, Rinaldo, Roald, Ronald

Reuben (Hebrew) behold a son
Also Rube, Ruben

Rex (Latin) king

Reynard (Old German) mighty and hardy
Also Raynard, Reinhard, Renard, Renaud, Rennard

Rhys *see* Reece

Richard (Old German) hard ruler
Also Rhicert, Rhisiart, Ricard, Ricardo, Riccardo, Richardus, Richart, Richerd, Riocart, Ryszard

Roald (Norwegian) *see* Reginald

Robert (Old German) bright
shining fame
Also Bob, Hrodebert, Riobard,
Roberto, Robertson, Robertus,
Robin, Robinson, Rupert,
Ruperto, Ruprecht

Robin *see* Robert

Rock (Old English) a rock

Roderick (Old German) famous
ruler
Also Roderich, Roderigo,
Roderikus, Rodrigo, Rodrigue,
Ruaidhri, Ruik

Rodney (English) a place name

Roger (Old English) famous
spear
Also Rodger, Rogerio, Rogero,
Rogier, Rudigar, Ruggiero,
Rutger

Roland (Old German) fame of
the land
Also Orlando, Rodhlann,
Roeland, Rolando, Roldan,
Rollan, Rolland, Rollin,
Rowland

Ronald (Scottish) *see* Reginald

Rory (Irish) red or ruddy

Roscoe (Old Norse) from the
deer forest

Ross (Scotch Gaelic) from the
peninsula

Rowan (Scandinavian)
mountain ash tree

Roy (French) king
Also Rey, Roi, Ruy

Rudolph (Old German) famous
wolf
Also Hrudolf, Rodolf, Rodolfo,
Rodolph, Rodolphe, Rudolf,
Rudolfe

Rudyard (Old English) from the
red enclosure

Rufus (Latin) red-haired one

Rupert *see* Robert

Russell (Latin) red or rusty

Ryan (Irish) little king
Also Rhien

S

Sacheverell (Old French) kid gloves

Salvador (Spanish) the saviour
Also Salvadore, Salvator, Sauveur, Xavier

Samson (Hebrew) like the sun
Also Sampson, Sansom, Sanson, Sansone, Simpson

Samuel (Hebrew) heard by God
Also Samhairle, Sammel, Samuele

Sancho (Spanish) sanctified or holy
Also Santo

Sandy *see* Alexander

Saul (Hebrew) the asked or longed for

Scott (Old English) a Scotsman
Also Scotti

Seamus (Irish) *see* James

Sean (Irish) *see* John

Sebastian (Latin) the revered one
Also Bastian, Bastien, Sebastiano, Sebastien

Seth (Hebrew) substitute or compensation

Shane *see* John

Shannon (Irish) little old wise one

Sheridan (Irish) wild man

Sherlock (Old English) fair-haired, clear lake

Shiro (Japanese) fourth son

Shu-sai-chong (Chinese) happy all his life long

Sidney (Old English) from St Denis
Also Sydney

Siegfried (Old German) peaceful victory
Also Siffre, Sigfrid, Sigvard

Sigmund (Old German) protecting conqueror
Also Sigismond, Sigismund, Sigismundo, Sigismundus, Sygmunt

Silas (Latin) of the forest

Silvester (Latin) woody, from the forest
Also Sailbheastar, Silvestre, Silvestro, Sylvester

Simon (Greek) one who hears
Also Sim, Simeon, Simone, Siomonn

Sinclair (English) shining light

Solomon (Hebrew) peaceful
Also Salomo, Salomon,
Solamh, Salamon, Soloman,
Solomone

Spencer (Old French)
dispenser of provisions or
storekeeper

Spiro (Greek) breath of the
gods

Stanford (Old English) dweller
by the stony ford

Stanislaus (Slavonic) one who
stands gloriously
Also Aineislis, Stanislas,
Stanislav

Stanley (Old English) from the
stony meadow
Also Stanleigh, Stanly

Stephen (Greek) crown or
garland
Also Esteban, Estevan,
Etienne, Istvan, Steaphan,
Stefan, Stefano, Steffen,
Stephanos, Stephanus,
Stephenson, Steven,
Stevenson

Stewart (Old English) steward
or tender of the estate
Also Stuart

Sumner (English) one who
summons by authority
Also Sumnor

Swain (Old German) a young
man or boy in service

Sydney *see* Sidney

Sylvester *see* Silvester

T

Taber (Gaelic) a spring well

Tabor (Turkish) fortified encampment

Taffy (Welsh) *see* David

Talbot (Old English) a woodcutter
Also Talbott

Tancred (Old German) considered counsel

Tate (Middle English) cheerful or joyful one
Also Tait

Taylor (English) occupational name

Ted/Teddy *see* Edward

Terence (Latin) smooth, polished one
Also Terencio, Terenz, Terry, Thierry

Thaddeus (Aramaic) praiser (Greek) stout-hearted, courageous
Also Taddeo, Tadeo, Tadhg, Thaddaus

Thane (Old English) courtier

Thanh (Vietnamese) tranquil, serene

Theobald (Old German) bold people

Theodore (Greek) God's gift
Also Feodor, Fyodor, Teodoro, Theodor, Theodous, Tudor

Thierry (French) *see* Terence

Thomas (Aramaic) a twin
Also Tamas, Tammany, Tammen, Tomas, Tomaso, Tomaz, Tomlin, Tuomas

Thor (Old Norse) thunderer
Also Thorold, Tor

Thornton (Old English) thorny town

Thurston (Danish) Thor's stone or jewel

Tiernan (Celtic) kingly

Timothy (Greek) honour and respect for God

Titus (Greek) safe; honoured
Also Tito

Tobias (Old English) God is good
Also Tioboid, Tobia, Tobiasz, Tobie, Toby

Todd (English) a thicket

Tonio *see* Anthony

Tony *see* Anthony

Tracy (Latin) bold, courageous one

Also Tracey

Trahern (Welsh) strong as iron
  Also Tray

Travers (Old French) from the
  crossroads
  Also Travis

Travis *see* Travers

Tremayne (Old Cornish)
  dweller at the stony town

Trent (English) place name

Trevor (English) great
  homestead

Tristan (Latin) the sorrowing
  Also Drostan, Tristran

Tristram (Celtic) tumult or din

Troy (French) from the land of
  the people with curly hair

Tynan (Irish) dark

Tyrone (Greek) sovereign, land
  owner

U

Ulric (Old English) wolf
  ruler
  Also Ulrich
Ulysses (Greek) hater of
  injustice
Uri *see* Uriah

Uriah (Hebrew) the Lord is my
  light
  Also Uri, Uria, Uriel
Uriel *see* Uriah
Uzziah (Hebrew) the Lord gives
  strength

V

Valentine (Latin) valiant and strong one
Also Bailintin, Valentijn, Valentin, Valentino

Valerian (Latin) strong and healthy one
Also Valarius, Valerius, Valéry

Vance (Dutch) from
Also Van

Varian (Latin) capricious, changeable
Also Varien, Varion, Varrian

Vassily *see* Basil

Vaughan (Celtic) little man
Also Vaughn

Vernon (Latin) to grow green and flourish
Also Verne

Victor (Latin) victorious conquerer
Also Buadhach, Vitorio, Vittorio

Vincent (Latin) conquering
Also Vincente, Vincentio, Vincentius, Vincenty, Vincenz, Vinsionn

Virgil (Latin) flourishing
Also Virgilio, Virgio

Vito (Latin) alive, animated
Also Vitalis

Vivian (Latin) vital; alive
Also Ninian, Vivien

Vladimir (Old Slavonic) glory of princes

W

Wade (Old German) advancing

Walden (Old German–English) mighty ruler, usurper
Also Waldo

Wallace (Scottish) a Welshman
Also Wallache, Wallis, Walsh, Welch, Welsh

Walter (Old German) ruler of people
Also Galterius, Gauthier, Gautier, Gualterio, Gualtiero, Ualtar, Walther, Waltier

Walton (English) wall, rampart, fortified town
Also Wally, Walt

Ward (Old English) watchman, guardian
Also Warde

Warner (Old German) protecting warrior
Also Werner

Warren (Old German) watchman, protecting friend

Warwick (Old German) strong ruler and defender
Also Warrick

Wayne (Old English) wagon-maker

Wen (Chinese) cultured

Wesley (Old English) of the west meadow
Also Westleigh

Weylin (Celtic) son of the wolf

Wilbur (Old German) resolute and brilliant

Willard (Old German) strong-willed or determined

William (Old German) resolute protector
Also Guglielmo, Guilhermo, Guillaume, Guillermo, Gwylim, Liam, Quilliam, Uilliam, Vilhelm, Viljo, Ville, Wiley, Wilhelm, Wilkes, Wilkie, Willem, Willis

Willis (Old English) *see* William

Willoughby (Old English) dwelling beside willow tree

Wilmot (Old German) resolute spirit or heart

Winston (Old English) from a friend's estate

Wolcott (Old English) cottage in a field

Wolfe (Old English) a wolf

Wolfgang (Old German) advancing wolf, progressive

Wyatt (Old English) from 'gwy', water

Wylie (Old English) beguiling, charming

X Y Z

Xavier *see* Salvador

Xenophon (Greek) stranger's voice

Xenos (Greek) stranger

Xerxes (Persian) after King Xerxes I of Persia

Yael (Hebrew) strength of God

Yale (Old English) old

Yardley (English) enclosure, residence
Also Lee, Leigh

Yates (Old English) from the gates
Also Gates, Yeats

Yehudi (Hebrew) the praise of the Lord

Yemen (Japanese) guarding the gate

Yiannis *see* John

Yoland (Greek) the violet

Yule (Old Norse) Christmas time
Also Yul

Yun (Chinese) fair and just

Yuri (Russian) *see* George

Yves (French) the archer
Also Ives, Ivo

Zachary (Hebrew) God remembered
Also Zacarias, Zacarius, Zaccaria, Zacchaeus, Zachariah, Zacharias, Zacharie, Zakarias, Zakarij, Zechariah

Zenas (Greek) God's gift

Zephaniah (Hebrew) God is darkness

Zev (Hebrew) deer
Also Zevie, Zvi

MORE POCKET PENGUINS
published or forthcoming

Choosing a Name for Your Baby
Family First Aid
How to Make Over 200 Cocktails
Chess Made Easy
Removing Stains and Other Household Hints
Microwave Tips and Techniques
Speaking in Public
The Pocket Easy Speller
Book of Cat Names
Book of Dog Names